"Jason and Jessamin have giv
to help us understand more
of the issues that continue to
is a timely resource that every
multicultural context of world
recommend it enough."

.₁cad. I cannot

HARVEY KWIYANI, CEO, Global Connections

"'Will Christians respond to the current turmoil over race with "wise
actions" or as "passers-by"?' That is the question posed by the authors.
Drawing on wide-ranging biblical foundations, shrewd sociological
understanding and closely detailed personal experience they point us
to thoughtful and constructive ways ahead."

REVD JOHN ROOT, Blogger at *Out of Many, One People*

"Considered and thoughtful, this book nevertheless provides a powerful
challenge to our thinking on race and ethnicity in the church. A must-
read for all who long to see the church as a place of welcome for all."

GRAHAM MILLER, CEO, London City Mission

"In *Healing the Divides*, Jason Roach and Jessamin Birdsall deal with
the uncomfortable truth of racism in our churches. They offer insights
and practical ideas drawn from their own personal experiences.
They are to be commended for dealing with such an emotive and
divisive issue with sensitivity and candour, backed with clear biblical
references. This is a timely and much-needed contribution."

RAM GIDOOMAL CBE,
Chairman, South Asian Concern

"There are not many books written by evangelical Christians in the UK
context on racial justice and unity. *Healing the Divide* therefore fills a
gap that is missing in our evangelical mission theology. One of the
unique things about this book is the authors. One is a black British
male of Caribbean background; the other is a white American woman.
The authors' different perspectives and experiences illuminate and
animate the book."

REVD DR ISRAEL OLUWOLE OLOFINJANA,
Director, One People Commission, Evangelical Alliance

"As a Black Caribbean Pentecostal in the UK, I welcome this work as a helpful analytical tool that can be utilised in the engagement between Christians in mainstream and black-led churches—the latter with their greater emphasis on agency and self-determination—as together we continue our Christian journey towards racial healing and wholeness."

BISHOP DR JOE ALDRED,
Retired Ecumenist, Churches Together in England,
Pentecostal and Multicultural Relations

"Jason and Jessamin help us to recognise our own cultural limitations, encouraging us to listen to those who are different from us. The book enables us to ask the hard questions about what it would really mean to be genuinely racially diverse as a church without simply expecting assimilation. I commend this book to you."

THE RT REVD & RT HON. DAME SARAH MULLALLY DBE,
The Bishop of London

"*Healing the Divides* is a brilliant little book. Meticulously researched by two impressive Christian influencers, it provides insightful, credible and balanced biblical assessments of race and class. All Christian leaders should make this book widely available within their sphere of influence and engage carefully and accountably with its key recommendations."

RICHARD CUNNINGHAM, Director, UCCF: The Christian Unions

"This book has a powerful purpose: to celebrate the ethnic diversity God intended and help bring about healing across the divides in British culture. Coming from diverse ethnic and class backgrounds and different genders, the authors are well placed to do that. So much about the authors' approach is striking: the stories they tell, the simplicity of the practical steps they offer to deepen relationships, the creative use of the Bible and the urge to prayer. The result is a book that challenges and encourages and has real potential to bring change."

ELAINE STORKEY, Consultant and lecturer in Social Science,
Philosophy and Theology

"The fair-minded, constructive guidance that Jason Roach and Jessamin Birdsall offer in this thoughtful, clearly-argued book will be of great value to faith leaders in their crucially important work for social justice. I highly recommend it."

ROBERT WUTHNOW, Princeton University

"This is a very timely, relevant and practical book on a very sensitive issue—it truly re-emphasises my own view that there is no perfect race but a race for perfection, and the true leaders in a nation are often the front runners in that race for perfection. I believe this book is a valuable reference point for the church and wider society."

ADE OMOOBA MBE,
Co-chair, National Church Leaders Forum

"*Healing the Divides* is important and timely. It shines the light of biblical theology into so much painful confusion about racial injustice and prejudice, especially for churches who claim we want the healthy diversity celebrated in Scripture but are struggling to make much progress. It avoids polarising extremes; it listens humbly for what we can learn from those we may not completely agree with; it provides a compelling agenda for change and the inspiring hope of God's heavenly church for all nations. I found it extremely sobering (so much I've got wrong), constructively illuminating (so much I didn't realise), graciously measured (so much gospel wisdom), and painfully challenging (so much I need to change about the way I think and do ministry). I will be urgently commending this book to our church leadership and church family. Thank you, God, for helping Jessamin and Jason write such a brilliant little book."

RICHARD COEKIN,
CEO, Co-Mission Church-Planting Network

"*Healing the Divides* is a biblically faithful, data-rich and culturally relevant challenge to the UK church regarding racial justice. It calls for repentance and practical steps to reconciliation with the hope of the gospel."

CLARE WILLIAMS, Founder, Get Real Apologetics

JASON ROACH AND JESSAMIN BIRDSALL

HEALING
THE
~~DIVIDES~~

HOW EVERY CHRISTIAN CAN ADVANCE GOD'S
VISION FOR RACIAL UNITY AND JUSTICE

Healing the Divides
© 2022 Jason Roach and Jessamin Birdsall.

Published by:
The Good Book Company

thegoodbook.com | thegoodbook.co.uk
thegoodbook.com.au | thegoodbook.co.nz | thegoodbook.co.in

ISBN: 9781784987275 | Printed in the UK

Design by Ben Woodcraft

CONTENTS

1. SURVEYING THE SCENE

Shock, sadness and shouts for **justice**[a] were just some of the responses reverberating around the globe as we started to write this book.

It was just a few months after the death of George Floyd (May 2020), which had catalysed protests against police brutality and racial inequality in the US, the UK, and many other countries. The disproportionate impact of COVID-19 on Black, Asian, and **minority ethnic**[b] communities in the UK had also put issues of **race** on the front page of newspapers and at the centre of public debates. Our hearts were heavy as we were swept up, in different ways, in all that was going on around us.

---

a Key words are marked in grey when they first appear and are explained in the glossary towards the back.

b At the time of writing, "minority ethnic" is the preferred term for describing non-white ethnic groups in the UK. Language is always changing, and any summarising term has weaknesses. We acknowledge this and encourage readers to use language that is as personal and specific as possible in everyday speech.

The increased attention to **racism** prompted many minority-ethnic individuals to speak up about their own experiences. I (Jason) was one of them—speaking out publicly for the first time about my experiences of racism perpetrated by police and people in the pew, both in the past and in the present.

Within a short period of time, racism became a more prominent social concern in the public eye. Thousands demonstrated in support of the **Black Lives Matter** (BLM) movement. Schools, businesses, government departments and churches publicly affirmed their support for racial equality and pledged further change. Articles, books, podcasts and special events directed our attention to the problem of racism and urged us to take action. But the surge in attention to racism then triggered a backlash in the form of attacks on "**Critical Race Theory**". Accusations were made that **anti-racism** work is part of a dangerous "**woke** culture".

How are we as Christians to make sense of these debates? How are we to respond?

The aim of this book is not to solve all the issues in the debate about racism. It is to offer fellow Christians some tools and frameworks to help all of us more thoughtfully navigate conversations about race and to better love our brothers and sisters of all ethnicities.

For some who read this book, the conversation about race sparked by George Floyd's death has faded to a dim and distant memory. For others, the conversation is live and personal. Some of us may be hurting because of the racism that we have personally experienced. Others may be hurting because of racism that we have witnessed or that has affected those we care about. All of us can feel at a loss as to how to feel or act in the midst of the pain and injustice in our society.

When a paramedic arrives at the scene of an emergency, they are trained to ask the right questions and bring the right equipment so they can begin to put things right. They may not have all the answers, but their toolkit and training make a critical difference. We pray that this book might help us as Christians, when confronted by racism, to be more like a paramedic than a passer-by—to take wise action rather than simply keep our heads down and walk by.

OUR STORIES

We believe that the church is called to be a place where people of all **cultures**, languages, skin tones and histories can participate, grow and serve together.

We've both been conscious of the ways that race and culture shape our experience of church for a long time.

Jason: *I am Black British. I was born in London to parents from the island of Barbados in the Caribbean who had moved to the UK to work and study. The suburb where I grew up was predominantly white. This meant that, apart from my parents, I encountered very few people with brown skin who were in skilled professions such as medicine, engineering, teaching or banking. It wasn't until we started to visit Barbados that I became aware of how much this had affected my own thinking.*

I remember wondering how the plane I was on would actually be able to land on the island. Who would have built the runway? Subconsciously, my environment had caused me to doubt whether, apart from some exceptions like my parents, Black people had the competence to do these things. It seems almost unbelievable now that, despite the colour of my own skin, I might think this way. But it meant that my parents' decision to make Barbados a kind of second home for us was all the more precious. Those subconscious stereotypes quickly evaporated when we were immersed in a different place.

I was also very aware of being seen as an outsider on both sides of the Atlantic. My accent made me a novelty in the Caribbean, while my skin and hair made me a curiosity among my classmates in England.

My wife is white, and we are on an ongoing journey of working out what it looks like to raise children with mixed heritage in a sometimes hostile world. We have also had the privilege of planting an intentionally multi-ethnic church on an urban housing estate. Over the last decade we have learnt lots about seeking to minister in a multi-ethnic, multicultural, multigenerational environment, often from our mistakes.

Jessamin: *I am a white American. I was born in Tokyo and spent my childhood between Japan, California and Massachusetts. I had the chance to meet people from many parts of the world and transition between different cultures. Early on I realised that church is both enriched and complicated by ethnic diversity. As a kid, I loved singing in Japanese, hearing the faith-filled testimonies of our Nigerian friends, and eating Korean and Filipino food at the monthly bring-and-share lunch.*

But I also picked up on the fact that there were sometimes conflicts around leadership styles and tensions about how best to manage multiple languages in the service. I observed that a Black friend of ours called Dame experienced overt racism; I, on the other hand, would get special attention for having blue eyes and red hair.

As an adult, I worked in India for a few years, where the caste system intersects with skin colour and class in ways that profoundly impact how people live and worship. These experiences led me to pursue a PhD in sociology, focusing on religion, race and inequality. Two years into my PhD, the 2016 American presidential campaign exposed deep and ugly racial divisions in the American church, and most acutely in the evangelical church. I started doing research, both in the US and the UK, into how evangelicals think about race and what helps or hinders churches from becoming racially integrated. My personal desire is for the church to be a community of welcome and justice, a place of healing and wholeness that points to the reconciling power of Jesus.

Both of us acknowledge that we see these topics of racial justice and unity through particular lenses. Our own identities and experiences have been profoundly shaped by our families, friends, skin tones, educational opportunities, work contexts, cultural environments and church communities. We do not claim to have a comprehensive understanding of the complex issues that this book raises. Certainly, we both have much more to learn. However, we have endeavoured to write with integrity about some of the things we have learned so far, with the hope that it can be of help to others who also long for church to reflect God's heart for unity and diversity.

ACKNOWLEDGING COMPLEXITY

One of the unfortunate features of the current conversation around race is that it has become very polarised. At one extreme, there are people who seem to frame all of society's divisions and problems under the banner of "racism". At the other extreme, there are people who believe racism is not an issue at all.

Who is right? Is race the biggest social issue we should be paying attention to, or is it a non-issue?

Here, it's worth taking a moment to step back. In 2016, the news in the UK was completely dominated by the EU referendum. Brexit commentary focused on class, region and generation as the pressing divisions in British society. Rewind back to 2005 and the news was dominated by the 7/7 bombings, in which 52 people were killed and 700 injured by Islamic extremists. This was followed by an uptick in anti-Muslim sentiment. At that time, the political commentary cast religious and cultural divisions as the greatest threat to Britain.

So, what is the most serious division in British society? Race? Class? Region? Religion? Culture? In truth, all these factors can be, and are, sources of division and prejudice in our communities—and all of them will shape our own experience of life and the kinds of opportunities or challenges that we face.

The media highlight different issues at different times. Individuals gravitate towards particular causes based on their own experiences and identities. Yet as Christians, we shouldn't determine our engagement with social issues based merely on what the hot-button issue of the moment is or what is personally relevant to us. Instead, we should be willing to reflect more deeply on social issues through the lens of Scripture, with actual data, and in conversation with people who come from a range of perspectives.

In 2020, race was brought into focus. While race is not the only factor contributing to divisions and inequalities in our society, it is a very significant one that demands our attention and action. For some of us, 2020 was the first time that we had ever considered the subject of racism in Britain. For others, this was simply the latest episode in a lifelong struggle against racial injustice. Whatever our background, we have the opportunity and responsibility to reflect and learn and take steps towards racial justice and healing. How can we as Christians think well about race? How can we engage in the conversation in a way that is thoughtful, honest, compassionate and humble? How can we build church communities that are genuinely inclusive of people of different ethnic and racial identities? How can we promote racial justice and healing? These are some of the issues we'll unpack over the next few chapters.

DEFINITIONS

Another tricky thing about the current conversation around race is that there are lots of key terms that people define differently. For the sake of clarity, we want to be upfront about how we are using these words.

Race is a way of categorising people based on visible physical characteristics. When we meet someone for the first time, we quickly (and usually unconsciously) place that person in the category of "Asian", "white" or "Black" based on their skin colour, hair texture and facial features.[c] We may also make quick assumptions about that person's origins and about their temperament, personality and behaviour. For example, in Britain, seeing a modestly dressed woman with brown skin and brown hair might trigger the category "Asian", along with assumptions that the woman is socially conservative, Muslim, unathletic and from Bangladesh. In reality, the woman might be a gregarious and skilled athlete of Indian ethnicity whose family migrated from East Africa.

---

c The decision to capitalise "Black" in print is an ongoing subject of discussion. In brief, our reasoning is that capitalisation acknowledges a sociological reality and the need for respect. Sociologically, people with dark skin have endured centuries of oppression. The collective experience of oppression has generated a sense of shared history and solidarity, despite variations of ethnicity and culture. While strict evenhandedness would mean capitalising "White" as well, white people do not have this shared history of oppression and do not tend to identify as a group on the basis of their skin colour. In addition, "White" has long been capitalised by white supremacist hate groups.

The racial categories that we place people in are not based on biology. As human beings, we share 99.9% of our genetic makeup with all other human beings. The remaining 0.1% of genetic material does contain differences between us, but those differences do not neatly fall into racial categories. There is often more genetic variation within "races" than between them. Two individuals whom we label as "Black" might actually be more *dissimilar* to each other genetically than a "Black" person and a "white" person.[1]

If you travel to another country, you may notice that the racial labels used there are different from the ones we use in the UK, or mean different things. For example, in the UK the racial category "Asian" in everyday speech tends to refer to people of South Asian heritage, while in the US, the "Asian" category tends to refer to people of East Asian heritage. In Brazil, the census uses the racial categories of white, black, brown, yellow and indigenous; though in everyday life people also use the broader and more ambiguous category of *moreno* ("dark-skinned" or "dark-haired"). This demonstrates how racial categories depend on the history of a nation and how different groups have related to each other politically and economically over time.[2]

Our modern concept of race in the West emerged during the colonial period, as European powers developed a hierarchy of racial groups that justified slavery and exploitation. In other words, "race" is a human invention. The idea of multiple "races" has neither a biological nor theological reality. It does, however, have a very powerful sociological reality because it has been used to rank, exclude, and abuse people over multiple centuries.

As we will unpack in the next chapter, we believe that "ethnicity" offers a more biblical way of conceptualising differences between communities. However, throughout the book we pay serious attention to "race" as a category because it has had, and continues to have, major implications for the ways in which people are seen and treated. For this reason we will continue to use terms such as "race", "racial" and "racism".

Ethnicity refers to a sense of shared peoplehood that is typically linked to ancestry, culture and/or language. Ethnicity is often considered a more positive term than race because it does not have the same connotations of hierarchy and power relations. Also, while race is generally an *assigned* category (that is, placed onto people), ethnicity is generally an *asserted* identity (that is, recognised and claimed by people).

Racism refers to ideas, attitudes and actions that perpetuate the beliefs that racial categories are real, that some races are superior to others, and that individuals can be reduced to racial categories. Anyone, no matter what their skin colour is, can perpetuate racism. When a Jamaican customer assumes that the Chinese shop owner is greedy and untrustworthy, he is operating on racist stereotypes. When cosmetic companies sell skin-lightening products in India, they are perpetuating and profiting from the racist idea that lighter skin is better than darker skin. When a white homeowner chooses to rent her house to a white family rather than a Black family, she is acting on the belief that white tenants are more reliable than Black tenants.

Racism is expressed both by individuals and within structures, and can be conscious or unconscious. *Conscious individual-level racism* is the easiest for us to understand. If a white man vandalises the home of a Black family by spray painting a derogatory word on their front door, he is clearly demonstrating that he believes Black people to be distinct from and inferior to himself. The white man has made a conscious decision to show his antagonism in a way that causes harm.

However, an action does not have to be violent or deliberate to be racist. My (Jessamin) sister-in-law is Puerto Rican and is of mixed Spanish, West African and indigenous ancestry. She has darker skin and hair than my brother and their two children. One time when visiting a church in England with their children, she got into conversation with a member of the congregation there. It became clear from the woman's questions that she assumed my sister-in-law to be the nanny. The conversation didn't necessarily convey that the woman held a conscious negative belief about brown-skinned people. However, it did suggest that the woman associated brown skin with the role of nanny and assumed that my sister-in-law wasn't married to my white brother. This is an example of *unconscious individual racism*. The woman asking the questions probably didn't intend to cause harm to my sister-in-law. I doubt that she hated my sister-in-law. More likely, she had absorbed ideas about brown women—perhaps from films, TV or a previous encounter—that built up in her mind certain stereotypes. However, the effect of her questions was harmful, as it undermined my sister-in-law's role as wife, mother, and professional geneticist.

Sometimes we get hung up on motives. We think that if we didn't *mean* to cause harm to someone, then we shouldn't be held accountable. Motives are of course important, but it is very possible to cause harm even when it is not intended.

What about "institutional", "structural", or "systemic" racism? These terms can sometimes be confusing if they are poorly defined or when they are used to lump every bad thing in society under the banner of "racism". We should take care to understand what people mean when they use these terms, and not to automatically dismiss or embrace wholesale what they are saying.

In this book, we refer to **"institutional racism"** as ideas, attitudes and actions that become embedded in our institutions—such as the legal, education or political systems—so as to systematically disadvantage some racial groups while giving an advantage to other racial groups. Like individual racism, institutional racism can be conscious or unconscious. Extreme examples of conscious institutional racism are the Nazi regime, the Jim Crow segregation laws in the southern states of the USA, and apartheid in South Africa. In these cases, clearly formulated ideas about differences between racial groups and the undesirability of certain groups were translated directly into laws, policies, and state-sponsored violence that inflicted extreme damage on Jewish people, Black people and other minority **ethnic groups**.

It's easy to see the moral horror of these cases and to feel a sense of relief that these particular examples are in the past. However, institutional racism does persist. And it persists in Britain.

Consider the findings of the landmark Macpherson Report, which was the product of an investigation into the murder of Black British teenager Stephen Lawrence. The report cited extensive evidence to conclude that the Metropolitan Police force was institutionally racist in the following ways: the poor treatment of the victim's family and lack of urgency in dealing with the case, the disproportionate use of stop-and-search on Black people, the police's underreporting of "racially motivated crimes", and the failure of police training to prepare officers to deal with issues of racism.[3]

More recently, in 2018 the Windrush scandal exposed aspects of institutional racism within the UK's immigration policy. Members of the Windrush generation—who had emigrated to Britain during the 1940s, 50s and 60s—experienced from 2012 onwards loss of healthcare and housing, wrongful detainment and deportation, and the humiliation of being treated as illegal immigrants.[4]

BRITAIN'S RACIAL LANDSCAPE

What does the racial landscape of Britain look like now, and how did we get here? While many of the voices speaking on this come to us from across the Atlantic, it's important to point out that the racial landscape of Britain is different from that of the United States in several key ways.

First, America has had a substantial Black population since the 1600s because of the transatlantic slave trade. Britain, by contrast, never had a large number of slaves living within the borders of the British Isles. Minority ethnic groups didn't become a significant proportion of the population until after the Second World War, and that was largely due to immigration from the colonies (particularly the Caribbean and South Asia) to remedy post-war labour shortages in Britain.

Second, in addition to multiple centuries of slavery, American history also included nearly 100 years of Jim Crow laws, which enforced racial segregation of public schools, public transportation, restrooms, churches, drinking fountains and many other areas of life. Many of these laws remained in place until the civil rights movement of the 1950s and 1960s. This means that racial inequalities have been built into the legal, financial, geographic and institutional fabric of America over hundreds of years. Britain has not had this same type or duration of enforced segregation. Of course, Britain has its own forms of institutional racism (for example, within immigration policy and the criminal justice system), but solutions to these inequalities will probably need to be different to those in the US because of our different histories.

A third difference between the US and the UK is the relative proportions of different racial and ethnic groups in each nation. As of the 2011 Census, 86% of the UK population was classified as white, 6.8% as Asian, and 3.4% as Black. As of the 2010 Census, 72.4% of the American population was classified as white, 4.8% as Asian, and 12.6% as Black. (The US census also includes additional questions which identify the ethnic category of Hispanic—16.3% of the population. Hispanic people are spread across the white, Black, and "other" racial categories.)

It's significant that in Britain today, the largest minority group is people of Asian descent. Data from the Racial Disparity Audit reveal that for some outcomes, British Asians fare worse than Black British people. In addition to this, the Rushdie Affair (controversy around Salman Rushdie's novel *The Satanic Verses*), the 7/7 bombings and counter-terrorism have caused anti-Islamic sentiment to negatively affect attitudes towards Asians more generally. In other words, religious discrimination gets mixed in with racial discrimination.

These historical and demographic differences between the US and the UK mean that we should be careful about importing American theories or policies regarding race directly into the British context without first considering what applies and what does not apply.

After reading the paragraphs above, you might be thinking, "Well, racism has certainly been much worse in America than in Britain. I guess we don't have to worry about it very much."

While Britain might not have had the same forms of racism, we should not underestimate the role that Britain has played in developing the *ideas* that allowed racism to become entrenched all around the world. During the colonial era, Britain, along with other European powers, developed and spread the idea that Black people were inferior to white people. They used this idea to justify colonial exploitation and slavery. The profits from the transatlantic slave trade contributed substantially to Britain's economy.[5]

Unfortunately, some Christian missionaries provided theological backing for these ideas about "racial hierarchy". They argued that white Europeans were God's chosen ambassadors to bring civilisation to primitive, dark-skinned people. They claimed that Black people were inferior culturally and intellectually to white people, and that they therefore should be under white rule.[6] Colonial powers, supported by bogus scientific and theological ideas, constructed a "hierarchy of races" with white people at the top and Black people at the bottom.[7] In colonies like Trinidad or Fiji, where the British brought indentured labourers from India to work alongside enslaved Africans or dark-skinned indigenous people, Indians were placed in a middle position in the racial hierarchy. Centuries later the legacy of those practices, and the ideas that made them possible, live on.[8]

When we look at Britain today, we can be thankful that the country as a whole has made progress towards greater racial equality over the last 50 years. However, we also need to recognise that we still have a way to go to become a place where people of all backgrounds are treated with dignity and have equal opportunity to flourish. For instance, Caribbean pupils are about three times as likely to be permanently excluded from school as white British pupils.[9] Black people are six times as likely to be stopped and searched by the police compared to white people.[10] Median household wealth (based on 2016–2018 data) was £313,900 for white-British-headed households, £224,500 for Pakistani-headed households, and £34,300 for Black-African-headed households.[11] While the reasons behind these statistics are complex, they indicate that ethnicity and race continue to shape the challenges and opportunities that people face in life.

The Bible teaches us that every human is made in the image of God (Genesis 1:27). God calls us to advance the flourishing of our communities and every individual in our communities (Micah 6:8, Galatians 6:10). To do this well, we need to understand the barriers that people face on the basis of race, and work to remove those barriers.

RACISM IN THE CHURCH

What about racism in the church? Surely the family of God is not subject to these same problems today?

Sadly, the church is not immune to issues of prejudice and discrimination. When immigrants from the Caribbean, many of whom were Anglican, arrived in the 1950s and 60s, they expected to be welcomed into the "motherland" and its churches. Unfortunately, quite a few experienced a cold reception from the churches they visited.[12]

These experiences of racial exclusion still happen in our churches and Christian institutions today. In my (Jessamin's) research, I interviewed over 70 people of differing ethnic identities about their views and experiences around racial diversity in the church. I heard many stories of minority-ethnic people being misunderstood, sidelined and hurt in their congregations.

These issues were often particularly stark when it came to training for ministry or entering church leadership. One person of Caribbean heritage reflected:

> *I found the course really difficult, because I was the only Black person in the course … If you go to an educational institution and not one person is Black that teaches you anything, or is like you, that's quite an uncomfortable place … You're basically saying, "We're not going to really change for you. We're not going to make you feel welcome or part of it. You just have to fit into our mould, and if you don't, then, eh, nevermind, it wasn't for you."*

Another woman, also of Caribbean heritage, reflected on...

> *… the sense that I experienced as a BME [Black and Minority Ethnic] person — "We quite like one of those, but*

we don't really want you sort of too involved ... So yes, we got a lovely Black, person of colour here in our parish, she can connect with others, other people of colour." But I didn't feel I had the same freedoms and enjoyment to flourish.

In other words, the white people in leadership above her expected her to minister to other minority-ethnic people but did not trust her to make decisions or exercise spiritual leadership over white people. This is a theme that came up repeatedly in my research interviews with minority-ethnic Christians. Recent books, including Ben Lindsay's *We Need to Talk about Race*, also highlight the ongoing realities of discrimination in church.

It's important to recognise that these problems of discrimination and exclusion are not limited to Black/white divides. Organisations like South Asian Concern and South Asian Forum exist in part to support British churches in becoming more inclusive of people of South Asian descent, who also often do not feel at home in mainstream British churches. In chapter 5, we will examine some of the cultural and structural factors that make it difficult for our churches to fully integrate people of all ethnicities into the life and leadership of the church.

We know from Scripture that the church should not be this way. The Bible paints a picture of a multi-ethnic, multicultural people who worship God together, love each other, and jointly work towards the flourishing of the communities where they live. With prayer, humility, intentionality and the grace of God, it is possible to move closer to this vision.

WHERE WE ARE HEADING

So how will we proceed? One of the key things a paramedic does when they arrive on the scene of an emergency is to perform a primary survey: they get an idea of where the problem is, and that changes their approach to care. The first few chapters of this book serve as a kind of "primary survey" both of the factors impacting racism in the UK and of the Bible's teaching, which will affect how we engage with the issue on the ground in our churches.

In chapter 2, we will explore, from a biblical perspective, why ethnic diversity should be celebrated and cultivated and why racism must be rejected as a sin. As Christians, it is important that our beliefs and practices around race are shaped by God's vision for a multi-ethnic, multicultural community.

In chapter 3, we will consider some of the anti-racism approaches that are mobilising action both within and beyond the church. We will reflect on Black Lives Matter, Critical Race Theory and a couple of other ideas that shape current anti-racism movements. We will think about what we can learn from these ideas and movements, and how to engage constructively as Christians.

In chapter 4, we will bring class and culture into the picture. It's important to understand how these intersect with race so that we can love people well in our churches and communities.

In chapter 5, we will examine how the way that we "do church" can create or perpetuate racial divisions. We'll suggest ways in which particular theological convictions may inadvertently make building community harder, and therefore make racial unity even more difficult to achieve.

In chapters 6 and 7, we will consider what repentance and progress look like, for members of the majority culture and for members of the minority cultures. At the end we also include a glossary of key terms and recommended reading if you'd like to explore these issues further.

What we won't do is provide a comprehensive history of race in the UK or an in-depth "theory of race". Many other books have been written on those subjects. Our aim is to equip Christians in the UK with some ideas and tools to navigate the current conversation on race more thoughtfully and biblically. We hope that this little book can help to inform and motivate readers to act in ways that promote racial justice and unity. By "racial justice" we mean treating people with equal dignity and respect, protecting the rights of the vulnerable, and holding to account those who have caused harm on the basis of racism. By "racial unity" we mean actively acknowledging and embodying the truth that there is one human race, collectively reflecting the image of the triune God through our ethnic and cultural diversity. Racial unity cannot be fully achieved while racial injustice persists. "Healing" the wounds caused by degradation, exclusion and exploitation is needed for the church to fulfil its purpose of collectively displaying God's reconciling power in the world. Our focus in this book is local churches, but what we discuss will have implications for how we participate in our local communities and other spheres beyond the church. Second, while we hope to inspire and empower every Christian who reads this book to play their part in this work, we recognise that for deep and effective long-term change to happen, church leaders and decision-makers need to take the lead.

In our nation and in our churches, the wounds of racism are real and painful and demand our attention. So we encourage you to read prayerfully and humbly, ready to submit to God's word. There will be uncomfortable truths for all of us to hear. But rather than letting these wounds fester or deepen, let's try to diagnose the causes properly and take steps towards healing and wholeness.

QUESTIONS

- Growing up, what was your neighbourhood like? What were your schools like? What kinds of kids do you remember interacting with?

- Reflecting on your childhood, can you remember a moment when you became aware of differences based on ethnicity? What struck you in that situation? How did you feel?

- How much do you talk about issues around race and ethnicity in your church?

2. THE CALL TO CELEBRATE
ETHNICITY

I (Jason) will never forget my wedding day. The copious amounts of chocolate cake; walking into the venue to see pictures of me in school uniform that I thought I had destroyed. But mostly, you'll be glad to hear, what made the day memorable was the woman that I married.

Rachel's background is in some ways very different to mine. She grew up in an all-white clergy household in the north-east of England and then spent time in the Middle East. I grew up in an all-Black household in south-east London. But our wedding day was a miniature picture of what God is doing in the history of the universe: bringing all kinds of people together to delight in his Son.

Whatever differences Rachel and I had, they pale in comparison with the differences between the protagonists of one of the Bible's greatest love stories: Ruth and Boaz. Ruth was a Moabite woman who had arrived in Bethlehem with her deceased husband's mother, destitute and in despair. Boaz was an upstanding and wealthy Israelite man. To grasp the weight of the differences between them, you need to know that generations earlier the Moabite people had tried to curse the Israelites and had then led them astray by encouraging them to worship false gods (Numbers 25). Because of this, God had declared:

No Ammonite or Moabite or any of their descendants may enter the assembly of the LORD, not even in the tenth generation … Do not seek a treaty of friendship with them as long as you live. (Deuteronomy 23:3, 6)

Given this history between the two nations, the climax of the book of Ruth is one that we shouldn't see coming: Ruth and Boaz get married. How was that possible? Because Ruth had come to seek refuge in the God of Israel, and no one who does so is turned away. In doing so, she was reconciled to the people of God. Ruth and Boaz's wedding day served as a preview of the radical reconciliation God intended to bring about through his Son—a Moabite marrying a Israelite so that the Messiah, who would descend from this couple, would be intimately connected with Moabite blood.

Their wedding—and mine and Rachel's—pointed forward to a future where people of all cultures and colours will be part of the family of God through their marriage to the Lamb who was slain: the Lord Jesus Christ (Revelation 19:6-9; 7:9).

It may be that you've never heard the book of Ruth described along these lines. Despite the fact that the writer is at pains to point out Ruth's ethnicity (the phrase "the Moabite" occurs five times and "Moab" seven times in the book's four chapters), its importance from an ethnic perspective, at least in the preaching that we have heard, is often missed in British churches. I (Jason) include my own preaching on Ruth as one of the culprits! It is as if some strands of the church have been conditioned to see these details as less relevant to the grand narrative of salvation. However, ethnic reconciliation is one of the key fruits that God intended to make manifest through the gospel—so in this chapter, we're going to celebrate it fully.

ETHNICITY AND THE STORY OF SALVATION

The Bible reminds us from beginning to end that ethnicity plays a key part in God's glorious plan for the story of the world. To illustrate this, we'll focus on one key text: Acts 17:24-31, part of the apostle Paul's great evangelistic speech on Mars Hill in Athens. As theologian John Stott comments, since "ancient Athens was a centre of ethnic, cultural and religious pluralism", this passage reveals Paul's attitude to a "multi-ethnic, multicultural, multireligious situation".[13] The message he preaches is incredible:

> [24] *The God who made the world and everything in it is the Lord of heaven and earth and does not live in temples built by human hands.* [25] *And he is not served by human hands, as if he needed anything. Rather, he himself gives everyone*

life and breath and everything else. [26] From one man he made all the nations, that they should inhabit the whole earth; and he marked out their appointed times in history and the boundaries of their lands. [27] God did this so that they would seek him and perhaps reach out for him and find him, though he is not far from any one of us. [28] "For in him we live and move and have our being." As some of your own poets have said, "We are his offspring."

[29] Therefore since we are God's offspring, we should not think that the divine being is like gold or silver or stone— an image made by human design and skill. [30] In the past God overlooked such ignorance, but now he commands all people everywhere to repent. [31] For he has set a day when he will judge the world with justice by the man he has appointed. He has given proof of this to everyone by raising him from the dead. (Acts 17:24-31)

Given his multi-ethnic, multicultural audience, Paul explains how the God of the Bible created that diversity for the sake of his own glorious purposes in redemption. We'll unpack this briefly.

Creation: "From one man he made all the nations" (v 26)

Paul begins by explaining that every member of the human race is both fundamentally the same and stunningly different at the same time.

Same dignity

All of us are created by God and are utterly dependent on him for "life and breath and everything else" (v 25). More than that, we originate from a common ancestry: we are descended from "one man"—a phrase that brings to mind the very first man, made in the image of God, as described in Genesis:

> [26] *Then God said, "Let us make mankind in our image, in our likeness, so that they may rule over the fish in the sea and the birds in the sky, over the livestock and all the wild animals, and over all the creatures that move along the ground."*
>
> [27] *So God created mankind in his own image,*
>   *in the image of God he created them;*
>   *male and female he created them.*
>
> [28] *God blessed them and said to them, "Be fruitful and increase in number; fill the earth and subdue it. Rule over the fish in the sea and the birds in the sky and over every living creature that moves on the ground."*
>   *(Genesis 1:26-28)*

Notice how Paul is deliberately echoing these verses in Acts 17:26 when he says that we were made to "inhabit the whole earth". Here's the bottom line: all people created by God, despite their sin, are worthy of profound respect as they are made to be royal representatives of the living God (James 3:9-10).

Every few years athletes compete for the honour of representing their country in the Olympic Games. It is seen as an incredible privilege to be a sporting ambassador on the world stage. In a much greater way, God has given us the honour of being his ambassadors in the created world.

This honour extends to every human being. Just as Adam and Eve were made in God's image, so too are their descendants—we are all "his [God's] offspring" (Acts 17:28). And, as Paul makes clear, that includes "all the nations" (v 26). We all share this privileged status of being God's image-bearers.

Different ethnicities
The word "nations" (v 26) in the original Greek is *ethnos* (from which we get the word "ethnic"). Rather than pointing to a political grouping, the meaning here was much broader. A "nation" was a group of people with a shared sense of ancestry, geographic ties and cultural practices. Remember that Acts 17:26 says that God "*made* all the nations". In other words, he intended ethnic diversity as part of his grand plan of redemption all along—it wasn't an afterthought.

Perhaps one reason that God created many nations bearing his image was to show something of his majestic nature as the triune God—his unity in diversity as Father, Son and Holy Spirit. As humanity came gradually to fulfil God's mandate to "inhabit the whole earth" (Genesis 1:28, Acts 17:26), so *our* unity and diversity was meant to be an advert for God's.

What a contrast all of this is to the "race science" that was used to justify slavery, developed in part by Carl Linnaeus in 1758.[14] He divided humanity into four categories based on continent of origin and skin colour:

Table 1: Carl Linnaeus' classification of *Homo sapiens* in *Systema Naturae* 10th edition, 1758

Species	1	2	3	4	5
Americanus	Red, choleric and straight	Straight, black and thick hair; gaping nostrils; [freckled] face; beardless chin	Unyielding, cheerful, free	Paints himself in a maze of red lines	Governed by customary right
Europaeus	White, sanguine, muscular	Plenty of yellow hair; blue eyes	Light, wise, inventor	Protected by tight clothing	Governed by rites
Asiaticus	Sallow, melancholic, stiff	Blackish hair, dark eyes	Stern, haughty, greedy	Protected by loose garments	Governed by opinions
Africanus	Black, phlegmatic, lazy	Dark hair, with many twisting braids; silky skin; flat nose; swollen lips; Women [with] elongated labia; breasts lactating profusely.	Sly, sluggish, neglectful	Anoints himself with fat	Governed by choice [caprice]

Such thinking, which divides human beings into false categories and assigns moral value to those categories, is antithetical to the biblical teaching of the dignity and equal value of all people. It has not only been used as a tool of oppression in the past but has cemented stereotypes that continue to cause harm and division today. This is a stark example of human sin marring the beautiful picture of unity in diversity that humankind was meant to display.

Fall: "So that they would seek him" (v27a)

The need to "seek" God shows how much humanity has rejected God and ignored his voice. Our first parents turned away from God (Genesis 3:6); the people of Athens turned away from him too, choosing to worship idols instead (Acts 17:29). In fact, every human has turned away from God—including us. We do not naturally look for him or listen to him. Instead, like Adam and Eve, we refuse to accept that God's words are true and act as though they aren't.

One of the symptoms of not listening to the voice of God is that we refuse to believe that we are all made in the image of God, with equal worth and dignity. Instead, we experience a sense of fear and shame around other people (Genesis 3:7-8). This is the sinful root of racism and all relational strife. This is what causes people, as American pastor Thabiti Anyabwile once said, to walk into a room, see someone different and think, "Not like me, therefore nothing in common, therefore not safe, therefore not going to have a good time."[15] Refusing to recognise that all people are made in the image of God then opens the door to elevating or degrading and privileging or mistreating other people.

Scripture explicitly expands on this theme in the book of James when describing the sin of partiality. Partiality is treating some people preferentially and being prejudiced against others, purely on the basis of external characteristics:

¹ My brothers and sisters, believers in our glorious Lord Jesus Christ must not show favouritism. ² Suppose a man comes into your meeting wearing a gold ring and fine clothes, and a poor man in filthy old clothes also comes in. ³ If you show special attention to the man wearing fine clothes and say, "Here's a good seat for you," but say to the poor man, "You stand there" or "Sit on the floor by my feet," ⁴ have you not discriminated among yourselves and become judges with evil thoughts? (James 2:1-4)

Although James' focus is judgements we make on the basis of socioeconomic difference, his conclusions clearly apply to other judgements we make based on external characteristics, including assumed racial difference. These kinds of judgements are usually linked to stereotypes that we hold about groups of people, which are very powerful. Stereotypes place people in boxes, prevent us from treating people as individuals, and often cause us to distrust or distance ourselves from fellow human beings. An example would be my (Jason's) son, the only minority-ethnic boy in his class, being cast in the school play as a hip-hop DJ at Cinderella's ball. Given that everyone else was cast as aristocrats, this role played into stereotypes about status and behaviour. James highlights how prejudicial judgements and preferential treatment on the basis of external characteristics are sinful and inconsistent with the character of God (v 1, 4).

What makes partiality a problem is that it suggests that some are less worthy of kingdom privileges than others (v 4). In fact, none of us are naturally worthy of God's favour. Christ had to shed his blood for every member of the church (Acts 20:28; Romans 3:23-25). To make partiality a pattern of life is to bring ourselves under the judgment of God:

> *⁸ If you really keep the royal law found in Scripture, "Love your neighbour as yourself," you are doing right. ⁹ But if you show favouritism, you sin and are convicted by the law as law-breakers. ¹⁰ For whoever keeps the whole law and yet stumbles at just one point is guilty of breaking all of it.*
> *(James 2:8-10)*

Showing favouritism is incompatible with God's command to love our neighbour as ourselves. If partiality (and therefore racism) is against God's will for his people, then we cannot tolerate it.

Redemption: "And perhaps reach out for him and find him" (Acts 17:27b)
Human beings of all ethnicities were created to "find" and worship Christ. This intention is evident in God's promise to Abram that through him—a man of a specific place and ethnic identity—"all peoples [that is, all nations and people groups] on earth" would be blessed (Genesis 12:3).

The fulfilment of this promise to Abram is possible because of the cross. Paul explains in the book of Ephesians that before Jesus, non-Jews were "without hope and without God" (Ephesians 2:12). But because of the cross, Gentiles have now been "brought near [that is, reconciled to God] by the blood of Christ". But he then goes on to explain that we have not just been reconciled to God but to each other:

> *[14] For he [Christ] himself is our peace, who has made the two groups [Jews and Gentiles] one and has destroyed the barrier, the dividing wall of hostility, [15] by setting aside in his flesh the law with its commands and regulations. His purpose was to create in himself one new humanity out of the two, thus making peace, [16] and in one body to reconcile both of them to God through the cross, by which he put to death their hostility. (Ephesians 2:14–16)*

Paul uses a very vivid picture in verse 14. The place where people went to worship God in the 1st century was the temple in Jerusalem. Ancient historians describe a physical barrier separating the outer "Court of the Gentiles" from the inner "Court of the Israelites". Signs were posted in Latin and Greek warning Gentiles not to go further into the temple precincts under penalty of death. They were outsiders physically and spiritually. But Paul explains that when Jesus died on the cross, it was as if a spiritual bulldozer smashed down this wall between believers from different ethnic and cultural groups (v 14). Jesus created one new humanity (v 15), which is only possible because of his work on the cross (v 16).

This powerful image of a "new humanity" reaffirms that people of all ethnicities are equally precious in God's sight and that there is no room for racial prejudice or oppression in the kingdom of God.

Instead of looking at people who are different from us and saying, "Not like me, therefore nothing in common", we can say, "God has made us different and dignified".

Crucially, the work of Jesus in creating a new humanity does not erase the beauty of ethnic diversity. The book of Revelation gives us a glimpse of the final fulfilment of God's promise to bless all peoples of the earth through Abram's descendant, and it is gloriously multicultural:

After this I looked, and there before me was a great multitude that no one could count, from every nation, tribe, people and language, standing before the throne and before the Lamb. (Revelation 7:9)

The direction of Scripture strongly suggests that our beautiful distinctions of language and culture are preserved for eternity. In other words, God intends to preserve multi-ethnic worship. As Jesus says, "People will come from east and west and north and south, and will take their places at the feast in the kingdom of God" (Luke 13:29).

Just as the diversity within God is part of *his* brilliance, diversity in the new creation will be part of *its* brilliance.

Repentance: "Now he commands all people everywhere to repent" (Acts 17:30)

Having started by affirming the dignity of all nations in verse 26, Paul now challenges the nations' attitude to God. Though they owed their very life and being to God (v 28), their worship was centred on something other than him (v 29). They needed to repent—to turn from going their own way and instead submit to God's.

This is crucial: to "reach out for [God] and find him" and to participate in his new humanity, we must repent.

It is repentance and faith in Christ that ultimately saves, not our ethnicity. It is repentance and faith in Christ that ultimately cements us together relationally, not our ethnicity. Ultimately, if we are believers in Christ, we have more in common with someone who understands little about our culture but who is a Christian than we do with someone from a similar heritage who has the same history and likes the same food, music and clothing as us, but who is not a Christian.

This is why the focus of this book will be mainly on racial unity and justice within the church. Much of what we say is relevant outside of the church, but it is only when we repent of our sins and turn to Christ that true unity across difference can be achieved.

PURSUING JUSTICE IN THE "ALREADY, NOT YET"

In the previous section, working through Acts 17, we highlighted the narrative arc of ethnicity in the Bible's story of creation, fall, redemption and new creation. We are currently living in the "already, not yet" period between Christ's first and second coming. Jesus has shown his victory over the fall, but we continue to live in a fallen world, and redemption is still in process. The new-creation vision in Revelation 7:9 of perfect unity in ethnic diversity will not be fully realised until Christ comes again. So what should we do meanwhile? Should we just wait for Jesus to come back and make all things right? Or is there something for us to do here and now?

Yes, there is. We should be actively celebrating ethnic diversity and actively tackling racism in the church. To quote John Stott:

> *"It is simply impossible, with any shred of Christian integrity, to go on proclaiming that Jesus by his cross has abolished the old divisions and created a single humanity of love, while at the same time we are contradicting our message by tolerating racial or social or other barriers within our church fellowship."*[16]

And as we've already seen, there *are* real racial barriers in many of our churches. At a debate in the General Synod of the Church of England in 2020, the archbishop of Canterbury said in no uncertain terms that his denomination was "institutionally racist". The presidents of Churches Together in England said in 2021 that "we are painfully aware of the racism that blights the life of our churches".[17] We cannot jump to the celebration of unity in ethnic diversity without first dealing with racial injustice.

The Bible is clear that God loves justice. In fact, outside of the relationships within the Godhead, in the whole Old Testament justice is the only thing that God is said to love, apart from his chosen people.[18] For example:

For the LORD loves the just
  and will not forsake his faithful ones.
They will be protected for ever;
  the offspring of the wicked will perish.
                    (Psalm 37:28, see NIV footnote)

As God's people, we are called to pursue justice:

He has shown you, O mortal, what is good.
  And what does the LORD require of you?
To act justly and to love mercy
  and to walk humbly with your God. (Micah 6:8)

What does "justice" mean? And how does it apply to race and ethnicity? We hear the word a lot these days. "Social justice." "Climate justice." "Justice for X." "No justice, no peace." It's also a word that is all over the Bible. The Hebrew word *mishpat* refers to treating people equitably, protecting people's rights (especially those of the vulnerable), and holding to account those who do wrong and cause harm. The other Hebrew word translated as justice, *tzedakah*, is also often translated as "righteousness". The basic idea behind this word is right relationships: right relationships with God and right relationships with fellow human beings.[19] As the author Jessica Nicholas reminds us, the Old Testament contains numerous commands to "do justice", and "'doing justice' meant not only not doing wrong, but also actively doing right and restoring what is broken."[20] Restoring what is broken involves paying attention to the most vulnerable in society, who may be in special need of protection.

Deuteronomy 10 puts it this way:

[God] defends the cause of the fatherless and the widow, and loves the foreigner residing among you, giving them food and clothing. And you are to love those who are foreigners, for you yourselves were foreigners in Egypt.
(Deuteronomy 10:18-19)

And in Jeremiah 22:3:

This is what the LORD says: do what is just and right. Rescue from the hand of the oppressor the one who has been robbed. Do no wrong or violence to the foreigner, the fatherless or the widow, and do not shed innocent blood in this place.

These passages teach that doing justice looks like treating people with dignity and kindness (even showing love to them), addressing material needs and protecting the rights of vulnerable people. In the Old Testament, the categories of "fatherless", "foreigner" and "widow" are often used interchangeably in such passages to refer to people who are most vulnerable to exclusion and exploitation. In our modern society, people who have suffered from racism would fall into this biblical category. In our wider society and in our churches, minority-ethnic people have often suffered the injustices of disrespect, exclusion from material resources, abuse, and restricted power and influence. Thus, doing justice to our brothers and sisters who have suffered from racism means treating them with respect, addressing their material needs, holding accountable those who have mistreated them, and advocating for their wellbeing and inclusion.

We hope it is obvious at this point that doing justice to people who have suffered from racism is incompatible with a "colour-blind" approach. People who advocate a "colour-blind" approach say that in order to treat people with equality, it is necessary to ignore their colour. This is misguided as it ignores the reality that people are already treated differently because of their colour. Doing justice to those on the margins cannot ignore difference, but must be attentive to where difference is used to exclude, neglect or mistreat. Both James and Deuteronomy speak of the moral wrong of partiality and also call God's people to pay particular attention to the specific challenges that specific groups face (James 1:27 – 2:1; Deuteronomy 10:17-18).

Pursuing justice is not an optional extra in our discipleship. As we wait for Christ to return and restore creation for his people, we seek to become like him by pursuing justice for those on the margins for whom we are responsible. The Lord is scathing of those who think that they can worship God while neglecting injustices on their doorstep. For example, in Isaiah 1:15-17 we read:

> [15] When you spread out your hands in prayer, I hide my eyes from you; even when you offer many prayers, I am not listening. Your hands are full of blood! [16] Wash and make yourselves clean. Take your evil deeds out of my sight; stop doing wrong. [17] Learn to do right; seek justice. Defend the

oppressed. Take up the cause of the fatherless; plead the case of the widow.

The rest of this book will unpack what pursuing justice might look like. But sometimes moving too quickly towards solutions can make problems worse rather than better. We need to fully understand the problem so that we can move towards the right kinds of solutions. That's what the next three chapters seek to do.

CELEBRATE, DEFEND, PRAY, ANTICIPATE

A groom in his wedding speech does not pretend that his wife is just the same as every other woman. That would be ludicrous. Instead, he deliberately picks out those things that bring him joy and celebrates them. This is one way that he honours his wife. In a similar way, we're called to honour Christ and point to the wonder of his work by celebrating ethnic difference.

Yet, so often, not only have we failed to celebrate ethnic difference, but we have distorted ethnic difference into a basis for hierarchy, exclusion, abuse, and even violence. Minority ethnic groups have suffered great injustices, and as Christians we are called to right these wrongs and pursue wholeness.

Thankfully, we are not left to pursue this challenging call of racial justice and unity in our own strength. We are enabled by the power of the Holy Spirit (Galatians 5:22).

From beginning to end, ethnicity is part of God's redemptive purposes. Jesus shed his blood for the church

(Acts 20:28), a community in which ethnic and cultural barriers were broken down and a new Spirit-filled community put on display for the angels to marvel at (Ephesians 3:10). How will we celebrate it, defend it, pray for it and anticipate it?

QUESTIONS

- Does the theology of race discussed in this chapter sound familiar? Why / why not?

- To what extent does your church currently reflect the demographics of your local community?

- What excites you about the biblical vision for multi-ethnic church? What do you see as some of the barriers to that vision becoming a reality in your church?

3. BLACK LIVES MATTER, CRT AND ANTI-RACIST ACTIVISM

Recently, my wife returned from a few days of camping with two of my daughters. Camping has never really been my thing, and the war wounds that she had picked up reinforced my feeling. She was a shadow of her former self! Apart from the expected sleep deprivation, she'd managed to stumble, at pace, into a wooden pole hidden in the long grass, grazing her shin and—in the somersault and fall that followed—badly bruising her shoulder.

As I helped her limp inside, it turned out that the real pain was in fact in her other leg. She'd been bitten by some kind of insect, and it had left her ankle throbbing. We did the usual: bite cream, antihistamine, ibuprofen. But four days later the swelling made it difficult for her to get into her shoes. Her leg was clearly infected. The treatments we were using were never going to bring full healing. They helped a bit, but fundamentally, we were working with an incomplete diagnosis, and so our treatment was incomplete—it couldn't entirely solve the problem because it left whole aspects of it untouched.

In the wake of the murder of George Floyd, many people have tried to find ways of engaging with the issue of racism. One way has been to support the movement Black Lives Matter (BLM). Thousands took to the streets to march in the organised protests, or changed their online social media profiles to show solidarity with the movement. However, some commentators began to suggest that although the intentions of the organisation may have been good, their approach was wrong—that perhaps, like the way that we tried to treat my wife's leg infection, the movement might have been in danger of misdiagnosing the problem and so relying on an incomplete treatment solution.

In our experience, this backlash against BLM has led to two things. First, the initial concern that seemed to be expressed in the wake of George Floyd's death has, to some degree, been drowned out by criticism of the intentions of those calling for change. Second, people in our churches who want to engage with the issue of racism have been left confused as to where to turn.

The purpose of this chapter is to show how Christians can begin to think wisely about approaches to anti-racist activism that we encounter in secular spheres. We'll explore how some of these ideas might help our attempts at racial healing, while others might not. This chapter is by no means a comprehensive assessment of all anti-racist activism. Within what is a very broad set of movements, we'll only focus on some of the key concepts underlying BLM, as well as some of the ideas related to Critical Race Theory (CRT). We have chosen to focus on these two movements in part because they have attracted significant attention and controversy within our society and in the church. But our hope is that you'll be able to apply the principles in this chapter to all kinds of contemporary solutions to racial injustice, helping you to engage in a way that is framed by biblical truth.

WHAT IS BLACK LIVES MATTER?

Black Lives Matter was started by three Black, female activists in the US in 2013, following the acquittal of George Zimmerman, who fatally shot an unarmed Black teenager, Trayvon Martin. The hashtag #BlackLivesMatter asserted the dignity and value of Black lives in response to ongoing racial injustice and police brutality in the United States. Since 2013, BLM has grown and evolved into both an organisation and a broader social movement, with supporters active in numerous countries, including in the UK.

So what is it about BLM that some people have found worrying?

One objection is that the policy solutions BLM proposes extend beyond the issue of racial injustice. For example, among the demands listed on the UK BLM website are:

- an immediate reversal of all cuts made during austerity.

- an end to prison and police expansion.

- an end to all British military operations abroad, including in Iraq and Afghanistan and across Africa.[21]

Such policies amount to a detailed and wide-ranging political campaign. People who agree that racism is wrong could quite reasonably disagree with any of them.

When I (Jason) shared this fact with one of my daughters recently, she was shocked. Her teacher had only that week asked her class to write about an issue of injustice. The list of options that she wrote on the board for them to choose between read: sexism, homophobia, BLM. In other words, for that teacher, "BLM" was identical with "anti-racism". Indeed, for many people, saying, "I support BLM" is simply a way of saying, "I am against racial injustice". However, for others more closely affiliated with BLM as an organisation, saying "I support BLM" means endorsing a broader range of progressive social policies.

A second concern that critics have raised about BLM is its alleged links to Critical Race Theory. For example, during a six-hour debate in Parliament about Black History Month in October 2020, Minister for Women and Equalities Kemi Badenoch linked BLM and CRT, saying that both were promoting dangerous and divisive ideologies.[22]

It is important to recognise that CRT is an academic framework within legal studies, and that not all anti-racism literature or activism is linked to CRT. However, there are some key ideas within CRT that have influenced wider anti-racism movements like BLM. We have tried to provide a balanced summary of the core tenets of CRT in Table 3 at the end of this chapter—although, as these ideas have entered the mainstream, important nuance is often lost.

Perhaps what is most controversial for some is the working assumption that racism has been systematically embedded across institutions in ways that sustain white supremacy. The implication is that for any real change to happen, society needs something far more radical than a few nasty people to be nicer to minority-ethnic people. Instead, change requires a complete overhaul.[23][24]

In the midst of the confusion around these ideas, what are Christians to make of them?

A TREATMENT APPROVAL PROCESS

During the COVID-19 pandemic, many of us became far more familiar with the vaccine approval process than we had ever expected to. As the vaccines were developed and trialled, the two key issues were efficacy and safety: did the vaccines actually work, and were they safe from causing any serious side effects? Only then could they be approved for use.

Think of this chapter as a "treatment approval process" for approaches like BLM and CRT. When we line them up against the Bible's teaching, do such approaches offer the right treatment for the problem that we face, and are there are any serious unintended consequences that come from adopting them?

We recognise that addressing such a question needs a huge dose of humility. No author comes to issues like this from a neutral standpoint. We all have blind spots. However, we want to help you begin to navigate the confusion using three principles:

1. The ingredients are everywhere

2. Be open to another angle

3. Beware of bundles

PRINCIPLE 1: THE INGREDIENTS ARE EVERYWHERE

Principle 1 is to recognise that truth can come from secular sources. Some Christians have argued that the ideas behind BLM are rooted in non-Christian thinking. Does that automatically mean that these ideas are off limits? This first principle answers, "Not necessarily". All truth belongs to God, and we can value it and use it no matter where it comes from.

Children are often taught the story of the discovery of penicillin. Alexander Fleming returned from a holiday to discover his Petri dishes had been contaminated with dirt that had a phenomenal effect on a dangerous bacterium. An ingredient completely outside his frame of reference proved profoundly helpful. Just as we can find helpful chemicals everywhere—sometimes in unexpected places—we can find helpful truth everywhere.

The biblical principle that this stems from is called common grace—God's general kindness to all those who bear his image. In God's mercy, even people who do not acknowledge him enjoy blessings in our world:

[God] causes his sun to rise on the evil and the good, and sends rain on the righteous and the unrighteous.
(Matthew 5:45)

These blessings are not just material but intellectual too. For example, Paul teaches that humanity knows the truth, even if they choose to deny it (Romans 1:21). Yet sometimes, despite that denial, they live according to God's ways, with their consciences "defending them" (2:14-15). This passage reminds us that ideas that accord with biblical principles and serve the work of the church can originate from people who do not identify as Christians. The great theologian John Calvin put it this way:

If the Lord has willed that we be helped in physics, dialectic, mathematics, and the like disciplines, by the work and ministry of the ungodly, let us use this assistance.[25]

Of course, like all ideas, secular thought must be taken captive for Christ (2 Corinthians 10:5)—that is, subjected to the limits of the Christian gospel and worldview. But when it comes to approaches to race relations that we encounter in secular spheres, we shouldn't dismiss them merely because they are not explicit about being Christian. The question is: are these particular ideas consistent with Scripture or not?

Putting it into practice – institutional racism

Let's apply "ingredients are everywhere" to one of the ideas that BLM emphasises: institutional racism (sometimes called structural or systemic racism).[26]

This is the idea that racism in a society goes beyond the conscious individual hostility of individuals towards others and extends to unconscious bias in our personal attitudes as well as discrimination embedded in institutional processes. One helpful definition was articulated in the Macpherson Report, which investigated the police's response to the murder of Stephen Lawrence. It described institutional racism as...

[A] generalised tendency, particularly where any element of discretion is involved, whereby minorities may receive different and less favourable treatment than the majority. Such differential treatment need be neither conscious nor intentional, and it may be practised routinely by officers whose professionalism is exemplary in all other respects.[27]

In other words, the report suggested that racial prejudice, whether intentional or unintentional, had ended up systematically disadvantaging minority ethnic groups.

Is such a view consistent with the Bible? Acts 6:1-7 suggests that it is. This passage describes an incident in the early church, when it emerged that ethnically Greek Jewish widows in the early church were being neglected in the distribution of food. This was not, so far as we can tell, deliberate. Nevertheless it had emerged as a "generalised tendency" among people whose behaviour was otherwise exemplary.

That's not to say that the concept of "systemic racism" is the primary idea that Acts 6 is seeking to communicate. But this passage, when taken with the Bible's doctrine of sin more broadly, certainly suggests that racism can be consciously or unconsciously integrated into processes in ways that cause harm.

Practical implications

What difference does this observation make in the life of a local church? Here's one example. In my (Jason's) multi-ethnic church, we have a number of rotas, for example, for leading prayers, reading the Scriptures, welcoming and cooking food. Sometimes those who organise a rota can default to asking people that they know well to serve, assuming that they have competence that others may lack. Perceived differences of race or class can be attached to stereotypes about people's ability or willingness to serve.

As a leadership team, we've been thinking about whether this communicates what we truly believe about church. We don't just want to get the jobs done; we want to do them in a way that empowers and models to the whole congregation the diversity within our church family.

We also observed that the way that people were asked to serve could bias the outcome towards people with more middle-class backgrounds ending up on the rota: perhaps communicating via email as opposed to text, or asking for lots of notice of availability instead of operating a few days in advance. In our context, this tended to disadvantage those from a white working-class background. (We'll explore the link between race and class more in chapter 4.) These were not inherently bad practices, but they did mean that people who checked email less or were more spontaneous were less likely to get onto the rota.

As one solution, we asked those organising rotas to be prepared to ask someone as a backup ahead of time, but then ask someone else on the day who might be less likely to respond to communication in advance. This is a small way in which we hope to address one of the issues of bias that can creep into our everyday life as a church.

PRINCIPLE 2: BE OPEN TO ANOTHER ANGLE
Our first principle freed us to take insights from non-Christian sources and use them if they are consistent with Scripture. But, you might ask, if they are consistent with Scripture, why would we need the non-Christian source in the first place?

That brings us to our second principle: different ideas, even ones that we encounter outside of the Bible, can sometimes help us look at a problem differently, from another angle, to see a truth that was there all along but that we might have otherwise missed. To put this into practice, let's look at two ideas that have emerged from CRT: "interest convergence" and "intersectionality".

Putting it into practice – interest convergence

The concept of interest convergence arose from one of the founders of CRT, Derrick Bell. He suggested that progress on anti-discrimination law in America from the 1960s to 80s was shaped more by the political interests of the government at the time than it was by a genuine concern for racial injustice.

The evidence suggests that this was the case. In 1954 a landmark Supreme Court ruling (Brown v Board of Education) paved the way for the desegregation of America's schools. However, the move turned out to be largely driven by the government's desire "to improve its image in the eyes of the Third World", in the hope that these countries would side with democracy over communism.[28]

Once this political interest was met, the incentive to roll out desegregation nationwide slowed, with progress often seeming to go backwards rather than forwards. While positive change still happened, it transpired that the desire for desegregation was not as strong or as unanimous among lawmakers as it had first seemed.

We see similar trends in the Bible. For example, when Joseph ascended to the position of second in charge in Egypt, the idea that the Hebrew people could ever be oppressed would have seemed laughable (Genesis 41:37-45). After all, Joseph was the prime minister! However, whereas the pharaoh at that time saw Joseph's wisdom as a means of protecting the Egyptians from famine, a later pharaoh saw the growth of Joseph's people as a threat. The status quo radically changed from one of honouring the Hebrews to one of enslaving them. As an ethnic group, their status and safety was hugely dependent on whether the interests of those in power happened to coincide with the interests of those who were not.

Practical implications

The idea of interest convergence can shed helpful light on the way in which we go about seeking racial justice. Perhaps one area to reflect on is our motives. When we seek to make changes in our personal lives, churches or Christian organisations, are we doing that to merely appear more socially aware, so as to benefit our status, without actually acting in a way that would benefit victims of injustice?

In the film *The Hate U Give*, one of the main characters, a Black high-school student, gets upset when her private-school friends are keen to go on a BLM protest. Her frustration is with their reasons for wanting to get involved—namely, to miss a school test and appear "on trend". The whole activity does nothing for the problems unravelling on their doorstep but it makes them look good.

When we change our status on social media or write an article for the church magazine, preach a sermon or put out a diversity statement for our organisation, we need to ask: are our actions undergirded by a desire and a plan for practical action?

At an organisational level, whether or not we involve those from minority groups in our decisions is an acid test of our motivation for change. If we are wanting to merely *appear* to be doing the right thing, we'll give little thought to who actually has the decision-making power. Consultation will generally seem less important or might only be undertaken superficially. But if we are genuinely interested in addressing injustices, we'll want to ensure that minority voices who actually experience oppression in our context are not only heard but enabled to influence decisions. In so doing, we'll also be less likely to make the kinds of mistakes that come from not seeing certain aspects of the problem or only seeing them in a particular way.

Similarly, when a racist incident hits the deadlines, is our first thought to phone a friend to see how they are or to change our status on social media? When we put out a diversity statement, do we actually have an implementation plan in place to back up our rhetoric? When minority-group members point out areas for change in church life, do we take time to consider those openly and humbly? In these small ways we might avoid merely acting in ways that advance our own interests rather than the interests of those we claim to support.

Putting it into practice – intersectionality

A second insight from CRT that we find useful is the idea of intersectionality. Like the phrase "Critical Race Theory", intersectionality has become a charged and polarising term.

At its most basic level, intersectionality simply refers to the reality that as individuals, our identities and experiences are shaped by multiple dimensions of ourselves. For example, my (Jessamin's) experience of life is not only shaped by the fact that I am a woman but also by the fact that I am American, university educated, white and the daughter of missionaries to Japan. All of these facets of my life "intersect" to shape how people treat me and what kinds of opportunities or challenges I confront in life. The concept of intersectionality encourages us to recognise the complexity of people and their experiences. We cannot reduce individuals, or the obstacles they face, to a single facet of their identity (say, race or gender)

There is nothing in this basic idea that goes against Christian teaching. In fact, the Bible seems to draw our attention to the reality of intersectional issues repeatedly. In John 4, for example, Jesus interacts with a Samaritan woman. This woman's experience of exclusion from society is shaped by her status as a woman, a despised ethnic minority, and a person whose lifestyle has brought her into disrepute. These parts of her identity overlap and compound the shame that she experiences. These details are meant to point out how far Jesus is willing to go to connect with people whose various identities would normally make it difficult for them to connect with religious teachers.

The challenge is in how the term "intersectionality" is applied. Some people use the idea of intersectionality to suggest that people with multiple marginalised identities have the most moral authority, while those from "privileged" groups should be treated as suspect or disregarded completely. The gospel teaches us that whether we are privileged and powerful like Nicodemus, whom Jesus meets in John 3, or dealing with multiple layers of marginalisation like the Samaritan woman in John 4, we are all equally in need of God's grace and equally precious in his sight. In fact, the conclusion of the Samaritan people in John 4 makes this very point: "This man really is the Saviour of the world" (John 4:42).

Practical implications

The idea of intersectionality demonstrates the need to really understand the experiences of those in our communities and churches, rather than making generalisations that miss the complexity of the individuals we are relating to.

As a Black man who has had a high level of education, I (Jason) have been told by white colleagues that I am "not really Black"—as if being Black necessarily requires poor education or low intelligence. But when visiting family in the Caribbean, I can also feel shunned when I speak with a south London accent on the streets of Barbados. This creates a profound sense of dislocation that many second-generation Black British people would relate to. None of this can be discerned by noticing the colour of someone's skin but only in relationship with them. Intersectionality reminds us that we can't assume that there is a "one size fits all" checklist for how Black people understand themselves or are understood by others. We need to slow down and listen.

The insight of intersectionality also helps us to see that solving problems of racism will be complicated by the different histories and circumstances of different groups of people. To return to our example from earlier, a highly educated Black professional may not struggle to get on a church rota. But a Polish single mum with several children who loves the Lord may struggle to feel that she is welcome and has been invited to get involved. The barriers people face and the discrimination that they encounter are different, and the solutions are far more complicated than a "one size fits all" approach. We'll look at this more in the next chapter.

In summary, when we're open to other angles, concepts such as interest convergence and intersectionality allow us to see truths that were always there in the Scriptures, which we might miss otherwise. Again, such points are not necessarily the main thing being taught in those texts, but they are present and helpful. Nor does learning from an idea mean that we are automatically championing other concepts or causes that may be associated with it.

The question to ask is: does this idea help us see truth in the biblical material from a new angle, which we might have missed otherwise? If the answer is yes, then we are free to develop that idea biblically and to use it where it may be helpful.

PRINCIPLE 3: BEWARE OF BUNDLES

In some cases, individual ideas get bundled together in a bigger package of ideas called an ideology. Examples of ideologies include conservatism, socialism, liberalism, globalism, feminism and environmentalism. For people who are committed to an ideology, promoting and applying the principles of that ideology becomes the ultimate goal and the means by which we can be saved from the evils that we face in the world. From a Christian perspective, the wholesale embrace of an ideology can be a form of idolatry—taking created things (in this case, ideas) and making them ultimate things.

In the case of the BLM movement, individual ideas about racial injustice have become bundled up with ideas about economic systems, gender and sexuality, and foreign policy. Its UK website states that "we fight against racism, but also against capitalism and patriarchy because ALL Black lives matter".[29] Whichever parts of that you agree or disagree with, our point is simply that to support the full set of BLM demands is to support a broad collection of values and ideas.

Another example would be the BLM demand that the police be defunded (that is, have their funding cut) and prisons be abolished. These solutions are seeking to address real problems. Police violence and inequalities in sentencing continue to be areas of injustice that need to be addressed. However, these specific solutions overreach themselves and are likely to result in other, unintended consequences.

We need to recognise when movements bundle ideas together in this way. The resulting package could be like recommending a leg amputation for someone with diabetes; it might be the right thing in some cases, but as a blanket approach it misunderstands the root of the problem and so proposes a solution that goes wide of the mark. As Christians we need to be wary of investing wholesale in an approach that inadvertently causes damaging side effects.

Perhaps the biggest weakness of the BLM or CRT solutions is that they do not take into account the reality of our universal sinful nature, which lies behind all injustice. While these movements have done much to expose crucial issues of injustice, we must remember that no set of policies can ever fully root out sin. Any attempt to stamp out racism that ignores this truth will never be able to fully produce the outcomes that it seeks.

Practical implications

We believe that one of the reasons that BLM is popular among some Christians is that it offers steps for practical action. The BLM website says, "Our revolution is not a public-speaking tournament ... [but] the collective effort of revolutionaries to transform reality, to improve the concrete situation of the masses."[30]

A desire to seek justice in practical ways is very much part of the Christian calling too, as we saw in the previous chapter. So if some Christians worry that BLM is problematic, perhaps a question to ask ourselves is: to what extent are we providing practical alternatives? BLM is attractive because it offers an avenue towards racial justice that has perhaps too often been lacking in Christian communities.

BLM as a social movement and CRT as an academic framework are both specific pieces of a wider movement of anti-racist activism. There are many other ideas, individuals, and institutions involved in contemporary anti-racist activism—some of which align with BLM or CRT and some which don't. The principles we've talked about above can help us engage with all kinds of ideas and movements in our broader cultural contexts.

Another related example is how we respond to the ideas encompassed by the word "woke". Like BLM and CRT, "woke" has become a politically polarised term. Again, we would be wise to pause and think about what "woke" means, rather than immediately embracing it or rejecting it. The word itself was first used by African Americans to refer to being alert to and aware of racial injustice. This is a meaning that all Christians can support. However, the usage of "woke" has broadened in recent years to encompass a wider set of progressive causes. So, as with BLM or CRT or anything else, let's try to understand what people mean when they apply the label of "woke" so that we can engage with them in a way that is thoughtful and biblical.

PUTTING THE PRINCIPLES TOGETHER

We need to engage in conversations about race wisely and charitably. That's just as true whether we're chatting with friends and church members or reading the work of secular writers and commentators we'll never meet. It's worth having three words in mind as we engage with others: Cry, Concept or Creed.[31] These three words are meant to draw out differences in what a particular individual might be trying to communicate and how we might respond to that.

1. **A cry:** An expression of solidarity with a group of people or ideas primarily to show sympathy with their pain, rather than to necessarily agree with all of their methods or objectives.

2. **A concept:** A particular idea or argument that I can examine in the light of Scripture.

3. **A creed:** An explanation for everything that competes with the gospel as an alternative story of salvation—"if we just do this, the world will be well."

Table 2 shows how applying these distinctions might work out in relation to something like BLM.

Perhaps the takeaway point from all this is that we get much further in understanding and engaging with the social issues when we slow down and ask more carefully, "What do people actually mean by the words and concepts they are using?" This happens best when we take time to enter into dialogue and relationship with people.

We do well to carefully assess an idea in light of biblical truth rather than either adopting it without thinking or

Table 2: Putting ideas in the right categories

	Example	Key question	Answer
Cry	"All lives will not matter until Black Lives Matter!" (Tweet)	Is this coming from a desire to campaign for specific political outcomes or an expression of solidarity?	I might need more information, but this person might just mean, "My heart cries out for those who are oppressed right now: Black lives matter!"
Concept	"Fight oppression." (Placard at a BLM protest)	Does the Bible agree with this concept or not?	I may be hearing people with all kinds of views using this language—and I may disagree on precisely *how* to fight oppression— but the sentiment itself does in fact fit with biblical principles.
Creed	"We believe we can create a world without systemic violence and exploitation, where all can live full and free lives … Defund the police and invest in communities." (BLM "About Us" page)	Is this a way of seeing the world that competes with / conflicts with the gospel?	I might need more information, but as my primary lens for seeing the world, this view is in danger of conflicting with biblical categories like the universality of sin and the need for salvation through Jesus.

dismissing it out of hand. Let's drain the bathwater while keeping a firm hold of the baby!

All of this takes patience as we interact with others on the issue of racism. We need to keep checking if we have really understood what people are saying and if we are weighing that biblically or merely emotionally or perhaps politically. Patience might mean being slower to dismiss concepts as unbiblical without fully understanding what they are. But in the end, slowing down might serve to speed up our desire to heal the divides among us.

QUESTIONS

- Is there one insight from the BLM movement or CRT that you could apply in your own response to racial injustice?

- What next step might you take to learn more about anti-racist activism?

- How could your church encourage people to engage with anti-racism in a more thoughtful way?

Table 3: What is Critical Race Theory?

The Critical Race Theory movement is, according to its founders, "a collection of activists and scholars engaged in studying and transforming the relationship among race, racism, and power. The movement considers many of the same issues that conventional civil rights and ethnic studies discourses take up but places them in a broader perspective that includes economics, history, setting, group and self-interest, and emotions and the unconscious."[32] The basic tenets of Critical Race Theory, adapted from the words of some of the key writers and thinkers are:

1	**Racism is "ordinary not aberrational"**—In other words, it is the everyday experience of most minority-ethnic people in America. This "ordinariness" when it comes to racism benefits the dominant group because it lends itself towards maintaining the status quo. Policies aimed at formal equality (the same treatment for everyone) will only ever address the most blatant forms of discrimination.
2	**Interest convergence**—Racism advances the causes of white elites (materially) and the white working class (psychologically). As a result, there is little motivation to change it. Significant progress only happens when it serves the interests of the majority group.
3	**Race is a social construct**—Race is the product of social thought rather than any underlying biological reality. Common physical traits like skin colour or hair have little to do with higher traits like personality or morality. However, society consciously chooses to ignore this.
4	**Differential racialization**—The idea that different ethnic groups are profiled differently at different times. For example, "in one era, Muslims are somewhat exotic neighbours who go to mosques and pray several times a day—harmless but odd. A few years later, they emerge as security threats."[33]
5	**Intersectionality**—"No person has a single, easily stated, unitary identity. A white feminist may also be Jewish or working class or a single mother."[34] These different identities must be taken into account in understanding someone's personal experience of the world.

| 6 | **Unique voice of colour**—This thesis holds that the experience and history with oppression of Black, American Indian, Asian, and Latino writers enables them to shed light on issues that their white colleagues are unlikely to know about. "Minority status, in other words, brings with it a presumed competence to speak about race and racism."[35] |

Having laid out these six distinctives, it's also important to say that those involved in this movement are clear that "there is no canonical set of doctrines or methodologies to which we all subscribe … CRT scholarship differs in object, argument, accent and emphasis."[36] For this reason, we need to be careful to examine what any particular writer or individual is trying to say.

4. WHAT ABOUT CULTURE AND CLASS?

Chidozie and Michael are both teenagers at secondary school. Their teachers have fairly low expectations of them and often ignore them or talk down to them in class. They've both been stopped by the police multiple times, even though neither of them has ever committed a crime. Sometimes when they walk down the street, they notice white women clutching their handbags more tightly. When shopping for a new pair of headphones or trainers, both boys have been eyed closely by shop assistants to make sure they don't steal anything. All of these experiences they share in common. Why?

Because their skin is black. Based on their skin colour, Chidozie and Michael are stereotyped as being less intelligent and more likely to be aggressive and criminal. They might be very different to each other in personality, culture, aspirations or behaviour. But they have a shared experience of being labelled as "Black" and treated in line with the stereotypes attached to blackness.

If we were to dig a little deeper, we'd discover that there are actually a number of differences between the two boys, including the cultural contexts in which they have been raised. Chidozie's parents emigrated from Nigeria and own a successful business together. They have quite a few Nigerian neighbours and are members of a majority-Nigerian church, where they have good friends and maintain a sense of pride in and connection with Nigerian culture. Chidozie's mum and dad are both optimistic about life in Britain, and they believe that if their son works hard, he will end up better off than they are.

Michael's parents were both born in the UK, with their parents having migrated from Jamaica. Michael has been raised primarily by his mother, Michelle, who works as a nurse assistant in the NHS and also as a cleaner. She has had multiple experiences of harassment and abuse at work and has seen other Black colleagues (senior and junior) being mistreated or disregarded. While Michelle tells her son to focus on his schoolwork, she is more concerned about his safety. Having faced many obstacles and disappointments, Michelle doesn't believe that Michael will do much better than she has in life.

As Christians we are welcomed into the multi-ethnic, multi-cultural people of God. To make our churches and our communities into places where people of all backgrounds can belong and grow, we need to understand some of the barriers to making that happen. The differences between Michael's and Chidozie's circumstances remind us of the value of taking an intersectional approach to understanding the challenges and opportunities that people face. As we pointed out in the last chapter, the idea of "intersectionality" simply encourages us to recognise that our identities and experiences are shaped by multiple dimensions of ourselves. Both Michael and Chidozie encounter discrimination because they are Black. However, their experience of discrimination and their response to it will be shaped not only by their race but also by their culture and class.

UNDERSTANDING CULTURE IN BRITAIN

Christians sometimes speak about culture in simple binary terms—for example, a preacher who says that "the culture teaches us X but the Bible says Y". This suggests that the church is somehow outside of culture, and that culture is monolithic. While there is something we loosely call "majority culture" or "mainstream culture"— shaped mainly by white middle-class culture, with some elements absorbed from minority cultures—the reality is that Britain is made up of multiple cultures. There are suburban and estate cultures; working-class and middle-class cultures; South Asian, African and Caribbean cultures; Tamil, Igbo and Guyanese cultures. Different age groups have different cultures (Gen X compared to Gen Z, for example). Our churches don't stand outside of these cultures but are part of them and shaped by them.

So what is culture? Culture consists not only of beliefs and values but also practices, habits, styles and narratives.

Together, these things provide people with a sense of meaning and belonging. When we meet someone who shares a big part of our culture—who grew up listening to the same stories or songs, experienced similar parenting, went to the same kind of school, laughs at the same kinds of jokes or shares our aesthetic tastes—we tend to feel an immediate sense of connection and comfort. One Christian writer, Andy Crouch, describes culture as "making sense of the world" by "making something out of the world".[37] Our cultures shape our identities and help us to navigate the world we live in.

When people migrate to a new country, they face a tension between assimilating into the majority culture and retaining cultural distinction. Assimilation looks like adopting the stories, styles, standards and practices of the majority culture. It involves conforming to clothing fashions, adopting new accents and body language, absorbing the dominant ideas and standards, participating in mainstream institutions, and imitating the behaviour of those around you in order to be accepted.

For people migrating to the UK, there are social and economic advantages to assimilating into white British culture. Assimilation can make it easier to be accepted in some social networks, get jobs in particular sectors, and avoid conflict. But there are major losses as well: loss of identity, community, tradition, language and history. My (Jason) father spoke with a very formal English accent and never went out without a suit. He chose assimilation.

As a result, some of his family and friends considered him distant, different and even proud. The choices that he made to fit in and get ahead had relational consequences elsewhere that were difficult to navigate.

In every society, it's typical for the majority group to assume that their culture is normal and to expect minorities to conform to it. In general, minorities know much more about the majority culture than vice versa. Every day, minorities navigate schools, businesses and statutory agencies that are dominated by the majority culture, so they have to learn the cultural practices of the majority. By contrast, people in the majority don't have the same incentive to learn about cultures different to their own.

In British society, there's an added layer of pain in this dynamic between the white majority and minority ethnic groups. Even though the colonial era is over, the deep-seated idea that white British culture is superior to all others persists.

One very small example of this is that I (Jessamin) have been repeatedly told that I do not speak "proper English" because I'm American. While people often say this in a joking tone, it points to an underlying attitude that believes British English is the standard against which all other forms of English around the world should be evaluated. The jokes that we tell and the anecdotes that we use can often be laden with prejudices. How we use humour requires sensitivity, particularly in settings where our aim is to welcome diverse groups of people.

For minority-ethnic people (many of whom come from former colonies such as Pakistan, Bangladesh, India, Nigeria and Jamaica), assimilating into Britain is not only about participating in a majority culture but about participating in a culture that is regarded as superior to their own, and shedding their own "inferior" culture. This can be a psychologically distressing process, and one that people in the majority are sometimes completely oblivious to.

Malorie Blackman explores themes of culture and assimilation in her book *Noughts and Crosses*, which was made into a BBC drama. In her fictional version of Britain, the tables are turned, and the dominant culture has African roots, with white culture deemed inferior. Watching an episode of the drama is a powerful way of stepping into the shoes of a minority-ethnic individual who is expected to assimilate into a culture that is dominant and yet in many ways alien.

How does culture intersect with race?

In Britain, the racial labels of "white", "Black", or "Asian" are attached to people largely based on their physical attributes (usually skin colour, hair texture, and facial features). But people who have the same skin colour can have very different cultural identities. Culture intersects with race to shape the obstacles or opportunities people experience.

Let's return to Michael and Chidozie. How does their cultural context intersect with their race to shape their experiences?

Because Michael is a third-generation immigrant, the majority culture will be very familiar to him and to his parents. Compared to Chidozie, he's more likely to have a diverse social network and to date someone outside of his race. He's less likely to live or worship in an ethnic-specific space. This means he may have less access to social and emotional support from people who share his ethnic identity when he experiences the damaging effects of racism. The fact that Chidozie's parents are part of a Nigerian-majority church and have a number of Nigerian neighbours means that when Chidozie does face racism in white-majority spaces, he can benefit from the solidarity and cultural affirmation of Nigerian-majority social spaces. The elders in his church remind him to be proud of his Nigerian heritage.

Chidozie's parents, like many first-generation immigrants, entered Britain with a sense of optimism and determination, and with high expectations for their children. When Chidozie encounters racism at school, his parents encourage him to persevere and to work harder. They pay for a tutor to help him further improve his academic performance.

As a second-generation immigrant, Michael's mum is less idealistic about British society and the prospect of upward mobility. Michelle watched her own parents face racial discrimination and has had to deal with many similar struggles in her own life. When she hears that Michael is having a hard time at school, she is upset but not surprised. Even if she could afford to, she does not see much point in investing in a tutor because she is not convinced that it will change how Michael's teachers see him or treat him.

We can also imagine two women, Emily and Marta—one English and one a Polish immigrant. When seen walking down the street, both women will be categorised as white and therefore assumed by the majority culture to be non-threatening, relatively trustworthy, and part of mainstream British culture. This is a **privilege** that they share on the basis of their skin colour.

However, after they open their mouths, they are likely to receive different treatment. Marta's accent will identify her as a cultural outsider and may evoke stereotypes of exploiting the welfare system or "stealing" British jobs. Even if Marta is better educated than Emily, harder-working than Emily, and more eager to contribute to her neighbourhood than Emily, she will still be treated by many as suspect and of lower status.

These examples illustrate how people who are placed into the same racial category will have common experiences of stereotypes, which can be advantageous or disadvantageous. However, the nature and intensity of those (dis)advantages will vary as they intersect with culture. Cultural differences in parental attitudes, strength of ties to ethnic-specific spaces, accent, posture and many other factors influence the way that people are treated and the way that people respond to racism.

How the gospel helps us

How are we to make sense of cultural differences and divisions, as Christians?

First, we need to remember that cultural diversity is part of God's good plan for the world. Scripture affirms that *all* people are made in the image of God (Genesis 1:27); this is not confined to a particular cultural group. This means that every culture has elements that reflect God's image and should be celebrated. At the Tower of Babel, God responds to humans' move towards conformity by diversifying languages and scattering people to develop multiple cultures. The people of Israel were not ethnically homogenous but included Cushites[d] (Moses' wife), Canaanites (Rahab) and Moabites (Ruth). The Psalms also provide visions of a multi-ethnic people, from all nations of the earth, blessing God and receiving his blessing (Psalm 72).

On the other hand, in light of the fall, we know that every culture is distorted by sin. This means that every culture also has elements that are not in line with God's character, and that should be challenged in our Christian discipleship. This truth applies to middle-class white British culture as well—consider, for example, the focus on privacy and the hesitancy to extend hospitality, or the fact that money and sacrificial giving are rarely preached about in many white-majority churches. Our point here is not that the majority culture is worse and

---

d Cushites were an African people of darker skin.

minority cultures are better. The point is simply that every culture, including the majority culture, contains aspects that do not conform to biblical teaching. Often members of the majority culture need the most help to see this clearly.

We know from Scripture that God intends that his people will include people from all kinds of cultures. God says to Abraham that "all peoples on earth will be blessed through you" (Genesis 12:3b). The work of Jesus on the cross enabled the reconciliation of all people to himself and to each other, including across cultural and ethnic divides (Ephesians 2:14-18). And in Revelation 7:9 we see a picture of people from every "nation, tribe, people and language" worshipping God together. This means that wherever we have people of different cultures living side by side—as we do in virtually every part of the UK today—we should be able to find them worshipping side by side in the local church.

As Christians, we are called to make sacrifices to accommodate brothers and sisters who are culturally different to us, as long as none of those sacrifices go against biblical teaching. In the early church, Jewish Christians, many of whom valued the Mosaic traditions and laws in which they were raised, were taught not to expect Gentile believers to be circumcised (Acts 15:1-11) and were encouraged to eat Gentile foods that they had previously viewed as unclean (Acts 10). Gentile Christians, meanwhile, were encouraged to abstain from eating meat with blood in it or animals that had been strangled, as that was particularly offensive to those from a Jewish background (Acts 15:28-29). Notice that cultural sacrifice ran both ways. Both cultural groups had to make sacrifices in order to live out the gospel together. Such sacrifices were necessary to foster fellowship between Christians of different cultural backgrounds.

Practical implications

While all Christians should be prepared to make sacrifices out of love for other people, when we find ourselves members of the majority culture, we need to be especially mindful of this. Rather than assuming that others should always be happy to make sacrifices in order to blend in with us, we also need to be willing to sacrifice our cultural comfort as we learn from and respect others. This is particularly important when engaging with people who are exploring Christianity or are new disciples of Jesus. It would be wrong to suggest that people need to embrace Jesus *and* white British culture in order to be fully accepted in church.

Unlike in Acts 15, where mixing between Jews and Gentiles was new and differences were obvious and stark, we are very often blind to our own cultural distinctives. Even when they are pointed out, they seem ordinary and normal to us. Yet we are called to try and understand when it would be wise to sacrifice our norms for the sake of others. In 1 Corinthians 12 for example, the apostle Paul points out that the body of believers is made up of ethnically diverse (Jew and Greek) and socioeconomically diverse (slave and free) people (v 13). Because our unity is so precious, we are each to bestow greater honour on the ones that we think are less honourable (v 21-25).

Perhaps one practical way that we might do this is simply to keep in mind the phrase *cultural humility*. Some church leaders speak about becoming more *culturally competent*. The phrase *cultural humility* emphasises that we will never be fully competent at understanding the many cultures present in our communities and churches, but we can recognise our own limitations and listen to those who are culturally different to us.

This listening can take many forms. You could read novels and biographies written by people of different cultural backgrounds, or listen to a podcast hosted by someone of a culture different to yours. When getting to know people in your church and local community, be curious about their story—what their childhood neighbourhood was like, what their school experience was like, what some of their family holiday traditions were, what they like or find difficult about the church they attend.

Over time, these listening practices can give us insight into the stories and practices and values that are important to other people, help us to see more clearly the assumptions and weaknesses within our own culture, and increase our empathy for those who have experienced discrimination or exclusion because of cultural differences.

UNDERSTANDING CLASS IN BRITAIN

Having thought about culture, we now need to consider another powerful factor in British society: class. Conversations around racial inequalities often lead to the questions: Isn't the problem class rather than race? Isn't race more of an American problem and class the real issue in Britain?

While racial inequalities can't be reduced to class differences, recognising how the two intersect will help us to understand the opportunities and challenges that people encounter.

What is class and why does it matter?

There are a number of different ways of thinking about class. It's partly about financial disparities—some people have more income and assets than others. It's also about differences in education and occupation, which give people access to different kinds of opportunities, skills, and social networks. It's also about social status—how people are ranked and assigned value or prestige. Self-perception matters too. In surveys, researchers sometimes use a picture of a ladder, asking the respondent to point to the rung where they think they stand relative to others in society.

Finally, group identity and culture have to be taken into account. When we use the categories of "upper class" or "middle class" or "working class", we are referring to groups that have some shared priorities, aspirations, styles and habits.

Given all these different dimensions of class, we can see many ways in which class influences people's experience of the world and the way we relate to one another.

From a financial perspective, an obvious point is that people who are poorer can't access the same quantity or quality of goods as those with more money—whether that's decent housing, or tutoring for their kids, or a week away at a Christian festival. The fact that income inequality in Britain is increasing means that the divisions between the "haves" and the "have nots" are deepening.

People in lower-paid occupations often also have to deal with precarious contracts, unpredictable schedules, long hours at work to make ends meet, and poor working conditions. This makes it harder to develop routines, plan ahead (on a church rota, for example) or be regularly involved in children's schoolwork or church small groups.

Social status (both in terms of how people view you and how you view yourself) is a powerful driver of how confident you feel and what you aspire to. People who are perceived to be of a lower social status are often treated as less competent and less dependable, so less worthy of investment. These dynamics can generate inferiority and superiority complexes, as well as resentment of higher-status groups.

Finally, in Britain, cultural traits associated with class are a massive barrier to social integration and social mobility. Cultural differences in conversational style, emotional expressiveness, humour, accent, leisure activities, approach to dealing with conflict, and many other things can make it hard for people of different classes to relate to each other. In some cases, assimilating into the dominant group can be seen as an act of betrayal by friends or family. This is part of the reason why social networks in Britain are highly segregated along class lines. Efforts to move beyond this will take time and trust to overcome.

How does class intersect with race?

Let's go back to Chidozie and Michael. We've already reflected on how their cultural contexts affect the way that they experience and respond to racial discrimination. So what about class?

Chidozie's parents, as business owners, have the financial resources to hire tutors for their son when they learn that his teachers aren't helping him reach his potential. Michael's mum does not have this option as she is struggling to make ends meet. Chidozie's parents have control over their time and so are able to join a parent-teacher committee to advocate for their son and to be part of a church small group that provides emotional and spiritual support. Michelle's hours are out of her control, and so she has much less freedom to help her son with his homework, attend parent-teacher meetings or join a weekly Bible study that her friend has invited her to. As a Black woman working in lower-status jobs, Michelle experiences both class prejudice and racial prejudice from her co-workers and clients. These experiences have caused her to feel alienated, worn down and without much hope for the future. Michael picks up on these feelings. He expects people to look down on him, and he perceives that hard work doesn't necessarily lead to a better quality life.

We can also imagine the experiences of Sana and Noor, both daughters of Pakistani immigrants. In Britain, the appearance of Sana's and Noor's brown skin and modest clothing can trigger stereotypes—of being cultural outsiders with low educational or career aspirations, submissive to men, and with potential links to terrorism. On the basis of these stereotypes, Sana and Noor both experience people talking down to them, teachers monitoring their behaviour to detect signs of extremism, and peers excluding them from certain social activities. Both have to work harder than their white peers to prove to their teachers that they can be assertive, to demonstrate that they are loyal to Britain, and to show their peers that they enjoy many of the same fashions and activities as other kids their age. Because of their racial classification as "Asian", both girls experience these shared forms of discrimination and exclusion.

However, the two girls have different class positions that intensify or moderate the racial prejudice that they face. Noor's dad is a consultant in the NHS. Her family can afford to live in a more affluent and racially integrated suburb, where Noor has picked up a middle-class accent in the school she attends. Many of the parents of Noor's classmates are university educated and so are able to informally share tips on applying to university with

Noor's family. Sana's dad is a taxi driver. They live in a low-income neighbourhood with a high proportion of Pakistani immigrants and very few university-educated people. She has developed a working-class accent which is likely to disadvantage her later in navigating university or applying for jobs. Sana has very few connections to people who might be able to help her with job or university applications. While both Noor and Sana experience discrimination on the basis of their race, for Sana this discrimination is compounded by her lower-class position.

These examples demonstrate how the challenges and obstacles that minority-ethnic people face in Britain intersect with class-related barriers and prejudice. Minority-ethnic people in Britain are present at all levels of the class hierarchy. However, some ethnic groups are disproportionately represented within particular classes. These groups deal both with discrimination based on their race and discrimination based on their class.

How does the gospel help us?

Again, it's fundamental that all people are made in the image of God. Therefore, everyone deserves to be treated with dignity and respect, regardless of their class.

The Bible doesn't use the language of "class", but it does refer to rich and poor, and people of high status and low status. Scripture is clear that neither rich people nor poor people are inherently superior—and warns that since earthly wealth won't last for eternity, we're foolish to build our sense of worth on it. The book of James puts it this way:

> *⁹ Believers in humble circumstances ought to take pride in their high position. ¹⁰ But the rich should take pride in their humiliation—since they will pass away like a wild flower. ¹¹ For the sun rises with scorching heat and withers the plant; its blossom falls and its beauty is destroyed. In the same way, the rich will fade away even while they go about their business.*
>
> *¹² Blessed is the one who perseveres under trial because, having stood the test, that person will receive the crown of life that the Lord has promised to those who love him.*
>
> *(James 1:9–12)*

Within the church we are "one body," given one Spirit, regardless of our ethnic or socio-economic differences (1 Corinthians 12:12–13; Galatians 3:28; Colossians 3:11). Scripture warns the rich against becoming proud, greedy, and oppressive of the poor (Proverbs 22:22). And it warns the poor against becoming anxious, envious, or bitter (Matthew 6:25-34; Hebrews 13:5).

Scripture encourages work (2 Thessalonians 3:10), the generous sharing of resources (Hebrews 13:16), and justice for the poor who are exploited (Psalm 82:4; Ezekiel 18:5-9, 16-17). Meeting Jesus should radically alter what we do with our money, as it did for Zacchaeus:

> *Look, Lord! Here and now I give half of my possessions to the poor, and if I have cheated anybody out of anything, I will pay back four times the amount. (Luke 19:8)*

Practical implications

In the New Testament we see poor widows, ordinary fishermen, highly educated Pharisees, and wealthy kings put their trust in Jesus and get involved in the mission of Jesus. However, when we look in our churches, most of us probably see an overwhelmingly middle-class congregation and leadership.

The New Testament letters to the early church suggest that the dynamics of a diverse church membership raised huge practical challenges. But the solution wasn't to segregate into different cultural and economic groups but to apply the gospel to the context of each church. This suggests that we should ask hard questions about what it would mean to genuinely include different classes in our churches without simply expecting assimilation.

One obvious assumption that this challenges is the idea that only the well-educated and well-spoken should occupy positions of leadership in church. Think again of the apostle Peter. Was he university educated? Did he have a high-status job? Did he make loads of money? None of the above. As far as we know from the Gospel accounts, Peter was a commoner—an impetuous fisherman who was not particularly articulate or sophisticated in society's eyes. And yet Jesus chose him as an apostle and granted him authority to lead the church (Acts 4:13).

In much of the British evangelical church, and most acutely in the conservative evangelical Anglican church, we often assume that for a person to be a good teacher, role model, and spiritual authority, they must speak in a certain way and dress in a certain way and have been educated to a certain level. Our assumptions about what makes a good leader often equate to "middle-class-ness". But this is not what the Bible says qualifies someone for ministry. How might our churches transform and grow if we were willing to recognise the gifts and spiritual maturity of people who are not university educated but who live in a council flat?

JESUS: THE GREAT RECONCILER

All of us are profoundly shaped by our race, culture and class. These parts of our identity shape the way that we see ourselves, how other people treat us, the opportunities or challenges we face, and where we feel we belong. While we can't reduce racial prejudice and inequality to issues of class, they do interact with each other. For example, the lower a minority-ethnic individual's socioeconomic status, the more likely it is that they will experience exclusion and prejudice more frequently and feel it more acutely.[38]

At the same time, we've seen that the individual circumstances of people who may have exactly the same skin tone can be very different. We will make many mistakes—as individuals and churches—if we assume that all those from a particular racialised group will think the same way or share exactly the same cultural norms. Our challenge is to recognise the complexity of people. To do this we must enter into genuine relationships with love and curiosity, rather than reduce people to stereotypes.

In the next chapter, we'll think more about how these dynamics play out in the context of our churches. Our sin has turned differences into sources of exclusion and conflict, and there is much for us to reflect on and repent of. And yet we know that Jesus is the great reconciler. By the power of his Spirit, we can exercise the humility, forgiveness and courage required to become a reconciled people of justice and hope.

QUESTIONS

- When have you made an incorrect assumption about a person, based on their ethnicity? When has someone made a wrong assumption about you, based on your ethnicity? How did this make you feel?

- How much socioeconomic diversity is there in your church? Why do you think this is?

- In what ways do you sacrifice your own comfort at church so that people of other cultures feel welcome?

- How could your church involve people of different educational backgrounds in leadership?

5. BARRIERS WITHIN THE CHURCH

In 2016 the Olympic heptathlete Katarina Johnson-Thompson rebooted her life. Her Olympic dream in Rio that year had ended with her reaching sixth place, which by her standards was failure. She was wondering what to do next. Her answer was to move to Montpellier, France, where a new coach helped her rebuild her approach to each event from the ground up. In other words, she realised that there were some fundamental barriers—limiting factors in her approach—that were hindering her ability to reach her potential. Performing at her best for the watching world meant identifying those barriers and learning new ways of doing things. Her work paid off; in 2019 she became World Champion.

The church has a far higher calling than an Olympic athlete. Our task is to put on display God's glorious work of reconciliation between God and humanity, and between his people. What barriers might we need to recognise and address in order to better live out this incredible calling?

This task of putting God's reconciling work on display was set in motion at the very beginning of salvation history. God's promise of salvation was always meant to be a blessing for "all peoples" (Genesis 12:3). The prophets looked forward with great hope to a time when "many peoples" would stream into the "temple of ... God" (Isaiah 2:2-3). But how this would happen remained a mystery. However, as we saw in chapter 2, the New Testament makes clear that those who were once "separate from Christ, excluded from citizenship in Israel and foreigners to the covenants of the promise" have now been "brought near by the blood of Christ" in order to be *built up together* as a church (Ephesians 2:12, 22). The work of Christ brings us together, so that we might live and serve together.

Incredibly, being built up in local churches is meant to reveal God's purposes not just on earth but "to the rulers and authorities in the heavenly realms" as well (3:10)! In other words, God designed the church so that as different ethnic groups live, love and look to the Lord together, both heaven and earth get to glimpse his manifold wisdom.

This matters because seeking to love people well as a Christian cannot be separated from seeking to love people well *as a church*. Christ did not die to save random individuals living independent lives all over the globe. He died to win for himself *a people* (1 Peter 2:9) to be a light to the world (Matthew 5:14)—a people whose life together puts on display the power of the gospel to break down cultural barriers (Ephesians 3:2-11).

The church is so central to Christ's plans that it forms his body (3:6; 4:15). It is so pivotal in his purposes that his Spirit builds us together as a family or household (2:19-22). It is so profoundly precious to him that he has pledged to marry his bride (5:25-27). In short, Christ "gave himself up" *for the church* in order to showcase his reconciling power across racial, social and generational divides (5:25). The church is right at the heart of the saving purposes of God.

If this is God's plan for the church, what limits us in fulfilling it? For evangelicals in particular, there are some fundamental aspects of our approach to church that can hinder us from being communities that model racial unity and justice. How can we confront and address these barriers, so that we better display God's incredible work of reconciliation?

SIGNS OF DIVISION

In chapter 2 we outlined a biblical vision for celebrating ethnicity that we hope seemed pretty uncontroversial. And yet Justin Brierley, Theology and Apologetics Editor at Premier Christian radio, wrote recently:

> *The fact that the UK's major Christian events are either almost overwhelmingly white or black in attendance (and almost unaware of each other's existence) is a reflection of what is often going on at a local church level.*[39]

It is also true that class division is rife in the church. The bishop of Burnley, speaking of the Church of England, talked of a "middle-class establishment bandwagon" that failed to listen to the poor.[40]

We haven't personally surveyed the whole of the UK church. No doubt there are plenty of notable exceptions—and if your church is one of them, that's a wonderful reason to praise God. However, we and others have observed that there are some stark divides.

Even in churches where there *are* people with different heritages, these churches can sometimes be multi-coloured but not very multicultural. Consider a church that draws people from all over a city and is made up of mainly young professionals. Participants in this church may differ in skin colour but be very similar in social class and cultural preferences. Attendees are able to fit in easily because they are quite used to minimising racial dynamics and cultural differences as they interact in society. Nobody really has to make any great sacrifices, because their cultural preferences and class privileges are so similar to each other. Such a congregation is, functionally, mono-cultural.[e]

---

e In some contexts, as in large ethnically diverse cities, there is a sense in which the majority of the members of the community have voluntarily entered a new cosmopolitan culture, and some degree of assimilation is reasonable and in fact natural. People in these kinds of churches may prefer to identify as a Brit more than as being from Barbados or Bangladesh. They may well also accept that becoming a Christian alters their identity and therefore, for example, the type of music that they want to listen to. But we must ask if we are too quick to assume that the most God-honouring worship happens to conveniently coincide with our preferred cultural style. There are also some parts of the UK where there may be less apparent ethnic diversity than in other areas. In situations like this, we are not called to seek out what does not exist or bus people in from other areas outside of our own local community! However, while ethnic diversity may be less common, class differences may be more so. In these

This chapter explores the factors in church life that can hinder churches from becoming truly multicultural and racially integrated. Whereas chapter 3 looked at what we can learn from secular approaches to racism, and chapter 4 focused on how we must take culture and class into account, this chapter turns the magnifying glass squarely on the way we do things as a church.

To be clear though, this chapter is not "ten things to do to improve church life". We get to something a bit like that in chapters 6 and 7. It's more like "two things about the way we do church that make racial unity much harder to achieve". It's important to be aware of these barriers because otherwise, like Katarina Johnson-Thompson, we could invest lots of time and energy in trying to pursue our goal (in this case, racial unity and justice) without recognising some foundational barriers that are making it more difficult to achieve.

We want to reflect on two barriers to racial unity and justice:

1. Our limited understanding of sin

2. Our individualistic approach to discipleship

1. OUR LIMITED UNDERSTANDING OF SIN

Every Christian can agree that racism is a sin. But our first barrier to working towards racial unity and justice is

---

contexts—which may appear superficially more monochrome—it is still worth asking whether the church community reflects, or is seeking to reflect, other diversities, such as class, in the local area.

our tendency to think of it as either mostly an individual problem or mostly a structural problem. These two viewpoints so significantly shape our approach to racism that we've taken time to unpack them in more detail in an appendix. In short, "individualists" believe that racism is mainly the result of people's individual actions and would be solved if we could all simply make the right choices. "Structuralists" believe that racism is mainly a structural problem that requires a dismantling of institutions and a rebalancing of power among decision makers for any real progress to be made (see Table 4).

The conversation between these two groups in wider society has become increasingly polarised, and this spills over into the life of the local church. An individualist might be quick to ignore, scorn or shut down any suggestions that church committees should be intentionally ethnically diverse. Individualists would say, "It's the behaviour of individual people that matters, not the composition of committees."

On the other hand, structuralists are likely to dismiss the potential impact of cross-cultural friendships on the life of the local church. "A few people having friends of different ethnicities won't make any difference to church culture or the way things get done," a structuralist might say. Both groups can become wary and dismissive of the other. Direct dialogue can quickly become strained as they seem to talk past one another. This makes the pursuit of racial unity and justice difficult because people are

Table 4: Two perspectives on racism

	Structural	Individual
Where is the problem?	Societal systems	Personal interactions
How big is the problem?	Big	Small
What is the solution to the problem?	Dismantling and rebuilding institutions Redistribution of power	Clarifying and enforcing existing legislation Ensuring respect in interpersonal relationships
What action should we take?	Campaign for structural change	Treat everyone with respect and avoid saying/doing anything racist
Most attractive to	Minority group	Majority group
Biblical evidence	Acts 6:1-6	James 2:1-13
Weaknesses	Emphasis on structures and processes can downplay individual responsibility Minority-ethnic individuals bear very little responsibility Limited acknowledgement of universal sinful nature	Sceptical of blaming "structures" Limited engagement with the history of racism Underestimates how a long history of racism continues to affect our institutions, cultures and attitudes

coming from fundamentally different positions on what the problem is and how things can change.

Perspectives in practice

Let's flesh this out with another example. One church that I (Jason) attended occasionally put on events that involved food stalls from different countries so that people from the church and their guests could enjoy them. However, despite there being a significant number of church members from Caribbean and African backgrounds, food from these parts of the world was never included. This was despite this fact being brought to the attention of the leadership and the event organisers on more than one occasion. An individualist might put this down to the individual organisers being forgetful and just needing another reminder. A structuralist might think that unless the people making the decisions change, the result will continue to be the same.

How the perspectives are linked

The idea that the problem of racism is either only individual or only structural is, however, flawed. The two things are inseparable. It is individuals who create structure, and structures that shape individuals. If sin distorts the attitudes and behaviours of individuals, it will distort the structures that they create. Sin then becomes embedded in structures, such that those structures continue to damage people long after their individual creators have gone.

One example of this in the life of the church can be seen in the way leaders are chosen. In the Church of England, for instance, there was undoubtedly bias against working-class people and minority groups in the way that ministers were selected in the past. Despite the widespread renunciation of such behaviour today, the current processes of selection nonetheless often reproduce the results of the past. Why is this?

An individualist might argue that since selection processes today are transparent, public and fair, we can therefore assume that, moving forward, the most qualified people will get the right jobs. Individualists might assert that there is no evidence of the sin of racism in leadership selection because there is no explicit rejection of candidates on the basis of race.

Structuralists, on the other hand, would claim that the sin of racism is embedded in the leadership-selection process because there are several factors that continue to bias selection in favour of white applicants and against minority applicants. These might include the places where roles are advertised, how information is shared, who sits on selection panels, how different kinds of work experience are weighted, unconscious expectations about dress and accent, and who holds decision-making power. In this way, the attitudes and actions of individuals in the past (which created an ethnically homogenous leadership) created processes and cultures that continue to produce racial disparities in leadership today. A structuralist would push for more concerted efforts to change these factors.

Most of us lean towards favouring one perspective (either the individualist or the structuralist) over the other. As a generalisation, members of the majority group (white British people in our context) tend to have a more individualist view on racism, while members of minority groups tend to have a more structuralist view. Polarised views on this can create a barrier to racial unity and justice in church because people struggle to agree on what the sin/injustice is, and therefore how to address it and move forward.

How our selfishness can distort our perspective

An over-reliance on either the individualist or the structuralist perspective may indicate that we ignore the tendency of our own hearts towards self-interest. The story of the first sin in Genesis 3 reminds us that we tend to want to divert blame towards others and away from ourselves. Adam blamed Eve for his disobedience, and Eve blamed the snake (Genesis 3:11-13).

Consider what it might mean if this same pattern was at work in how we tended to think about the causes of racism. What if our fallen instincts tend to cause us to default to a way of seeing the problem that removes any responsibility from ourselves? If there were even some truth in this, we might be wise to consider if there may be more truth in the "other" perspective on racism than we might be naturally wired to admit.

PRACTICAL IMPLICATIONS

Consider our biases

All of us, then, need to be aware of our own bias as we think about racism, and seek to learn what we can from the opposite perspective.

For individualists, for instance, this might result in simply being prepared to listen and not be dismissive when someone is speaking to you about, say, the legacy of colonialism, slavery and immigration legislation. It might mean resisting the temptation to recommend a book debunking "woke" culture as your first response. It might be as simple as not assuming that racism is somebody else's problem because you would never insult anyone. It might look like reflecting on where the legacy of past sins of racism are still experienced the most in your church and local area, and what you might be able to do about it.

For structuralists, on the other hand, being aware of your bias might mean giving more attention to the progress in equality and employment law in recent history—perhaps there is room for more optimism than you might normally allow for.

It might also result in asking more often, "What responsibility do I have in this situation to bring change?" It might mean being willing to invest in friendship with someone who is different from you, trusting that it could have an impact for others in the church life too. It could look like asking, "Am I walking into situations in church life assuming the worst from those in the majority culture around me and so appearing distant or sceptical?"

Critique versus compassion

It's also wise to reflect on where we put our energy as we address this topic. One danger is that we are drawn into spending all of our time critiquing wrong views, rather than working towards solutions. For evidence of this, take a look at Twitter on the issue of racism on any given day! It's true that if we have the wrong diagnosis, we will offer the world the wrong cure (as we outlined in chapter 3). But we mustn't draw attention away from the primary issue and so get side-tracked from actually developing and implementing the right plan. Perhaps a very simple question to ask would be, "When I feel I need to engage in debate on racism, how will my actions (both inside and outside of the debate) show that my desire is to help the marginalised?"

2. OUR INDIVIDUALISTIC APPROACH TO DISCIPLESHIP

The second barrier to racial unity and justice in our churches is our over-focus on the individual. Evangelicals are, perhaps, particularly prone to this. To be evangelical is commonly understood as a focus on the Bible, the cross, personal conversion and activism.[41] No one would ever say that community doesn't matter! But the distinctive priorities that define evangelicalism don't require it. To the extent that this is true, evangelicalism is a movement that tends to prioritise truth about personal salvation ahead of truth about the nature of the church.

There are at least two consequences of this that relate to race. First, it can lead to an individualistic community that is less likely to tolerate, much less celebrate, difference. Second, we can be disinterested in partnership with other churches, particularly when their cultural expression of faith is different from our own.

Individualistic communities

Evangelical churches can sometimes place a disproportionate emphasis on individual salvation and sanctification. We don't mean to imply in any way that individual salvation is not important! Only that the culture of church life can lean very heavily towards individual faith. For example, our community groups or Bible studies can often be relationally superficial and focused mainly on head knowledge. The idea of working towards deep friendships, let alone across ethnic differences, may not be seen as a priority.

If our spiritual growth is mainly about what works for us individually, we can also end up having a consumer attitude to church. What seems like a "good" church is one that suits our social preferences, tastes and interests as closely as possible. So, for example, if we have to move location for work and need to find a new church, we might gravitate towards a church where people share our level of education or lifestyle or ethnicity. This often results in mono-ethnic and monocultural churches, as a consumer attitude leads people to congregate with those they are most comfortable with as their highest priority.

However, as we've already said at the beginning of this chapter, the church is far more fundamental to the Christian life than our individualistic attitude suggests. In his letters, Paul highlights repeatedly his expectation that ethnic diversity will be a normal part of church life, when a church is formed in the midst of a diverse community:

> [12] *Just as a body, though one, has many parts, but all its many parts form one body, so it is with Christ.* [13] *For we were all baptised by one Spirit so as to form one body—*

*whether **Jews or Gentiles, slave or free**—and we were
all given the one Spirit to drink. [14] And so the body is not
made up of one part but of many ... and the parts that
we think are less honourable we treat with special honour.*
(1 Corinthians 12:12-14, 23)

PRACTICAL IMPLICATIONS

Here are some practical ways in which churches might
push back against our tendency towards individualism.

Re-examine our rituals

Many churches lean heavily towards treating the Lord's
Supper as a personal ritual, during which other people
just happen to be around. In doing so we miss out on the
fact that it also demonstrates the diverse community that
God is building through the work of the cross. The way
that bread and wine are distributed can help or hinder
this. Bread passed along a pew might feel very different
to a group of believers assembled at the front of church to
receive them together. Does the way that we facilitate and
speak about the Lord's Supper help people celebrate the
diverse community that Christ has enabled through the
cross and yearn for more of that?

Revamp our groups

In our small groups, could we review the balance between
social time and Bible study, both over an evening and over
the course of a year, so that there are more opportunities
for building meaningful relationships? Could we (so far
as the make-up of our church allows) intentionally make
the groups more ethnically and socially diverse? We have

both found that we have grown the most in small groups that are diverse in age, ethnicity, educational background and culture. Praying with people in different life circumstances helps us grow in compassion. Lamenting losses and hearing testimonies of God's goodness in difficult circumstances helps us grow in faith. Reading Scripture with people from different cultural perspectives deepens our understanding of God. Discipleship is about more than analysing Scripture; it's also about growing in generosity, compassion and wisdom, and bearing with one another.

Could we ensure that the theme of racial justice is tackled directly in such groups? This would give insight to those who are less familiar with the subject, and provide the opportunity to show empathy to, and lament with, those who are experiencing or have experienced specific struggles.

Read the Scriptures for corporate application

As we read the Scriptures, we could make a conscious effort to reflect on the difference it would make if its instructions and encouragements were applied to the whole church, rather than just to us personally. In the original language of the New Testament, there are two different words for "you", depending on whether it is an individual or a group being addressed—and very often in the Scriptures it is the plural "you" that is used. Deliberately seeking to read the Bible with this in mind opens us up to the demands and blessings of being in a diverse community. For example, I (Jason) am currently reading the book of James. Chapter 5 verse 8 reads, "You too, be patient and stand firm, because the Lord's coming is near." Treating the "you" as plural changes my application from "Lord, help me get through a tough day at the office" to "Help us as a community of believers to get through this season of difficulty we find ourselves in". For me to live out this second application, it matters who is in my community, how well I know them, and how we can encourage each other to keep going together.

Research the needs of your area

Connecting with the issues of justice that are affecting our local community is another potential way to combat our individualistic approach to church life. On the estate where I (Jason) have ministered for some years now, there have been multiple stabbings. Responding collectively to this trauma has created space for our community to mourn together, pray for those impacted and together seek change. Although we could have engaged with this issue individually, instead we have sought to put the spotlight on how we could work together for change and weep together over injustice.

Invest in partnership

I (Jason) heard one pastor reflect recently on how, when he planted a church, his narrative to the church and community sounded like this: "There were no real Christians doing anything useful in this area at all before now. Thank God that finally Jesus has raised my group up." This was not what he thought, but he recognised that this was how he may well have been perceived—particularly because he took little time to consult with other churches or the local community. He was honest enough to admit that part of this was caused by an undue arrogance about his particular formula for reaching the area.

The quicker a church is to see its ministry as the only valid expression of the Christian faith, the more likely it is that they will lean towards being ethnically and culturally homogenous, and the harder it will become to build church communities where ethnic and cultural differences are celebrated, or even only endured. If we feel that our expression of church is uniquely equipped to bless the neighbourhood, we'll be less inclined to listen to, pray with, support and partner with others, potentially missing out on opportunities to build relationships of trust and model unity.

So, in your area, could you form a relationship with another local church (particularly one with leadership of a different ethnicity to yours) in order to pray—and perhaps more? You may disagree on secondary things (and might even choose to articulate that to your church), but could you model a generosity towards them? This generosity towards the theology and practice of other churches on secondary issues, even if everything is not exactly as we would do it, might in turn help members within your church to reflect on their attitude towards their own church, as well as towards others. As Harvey Kwiyani puts it:

British churches cannot say to African churches, "We have no need of you." Neither of course can African churches say to Asian churches, "We can do without you."[42]

Whatever our context, could we seek ways of developing partnerships? If your local area seems to have little ethnic or cultural diversity, you could seek to form a partnership with a church further afield. Could you become prayer partners? Could you showcase their ministry at some point during the year? Could a connection with that church help you to display and celebrate the diversity that the New Testament talks about?

ONE BODY, ONE KINGDOM

Our intention in this chapter isn't to call into question all of our spiritual heritage as evangelicals or to pretend that there are easy answers. Instead, it is to highlight some of the barriers that can mean that our good intentions to enable racial unity can stall before they've even properly got going. These broader cultural barriers to diversity mean that we need to be *even more intentional* about cultivating ethnic diversity and tackling our larger cultural challenges.

The question at the root of the issues that we have discussed is this: how highly do we prize the fact that we are called to be part of a unified body? To quote one theologian: "Mankind is a unity ... one body with many members, one tree with many branches, one kingdom with many citizens."[43] Given this, we need to ask: How can we exercise our gifts for the common good (1 Corinthians

12:5-7)? What does it mean to love one another with a Christ-like love (John 13:34)?

Having said this, we return to a familiar but critical point. We don't put our hope in programmes but in the transforming power of the gospel. Sinners will naturally tend to separate themselves from others and find many ways to justify that. We need divine power to break the cycle. While we've outlined approaches to church life that could really make a difference in our desire to seek racial justice and unity, at the same time, we recognise that "unless the LORD builds the house, the builders labour in vain" (Psalm 127:1). We must continually look to the power of the Spirit to enable change in our churches, whatever our situation.

QUESTIONS

- Do you tend to think about racism as an individual problem or a structural problem? Why do you tend to think that way?

- How does the Bible's perspective challenge you in your thinking (e.g. Acts 6 and James 2)?

- What role do you feel you have in addressing racism?

- What practical steps could you take as a church to be less shaped by individualism in the life of your church community?

6. WHAT CHANGE LOOKS LIKE FOR THE MAJORITY CULTURE (JESSAMIN)

We've spent the last few chapters looking at the context around and barriers to racial unity and justice in evangelical churches in the UK. We've offered a few practical suggestions along the way, but this chapter and the following one are devoted entirely to practical steps we can take—as individuals, in our churches, and as our churches engage with our wider communities.

This chapter is directed at readers who are part of the dominant culture. In the UK, this means people who are white British. The next chapter is aimed at readers who are members of a minority ethnic group in the UK. There are several things that apply to all Christians, but quite a few that are specific to white people or to minority-ethnic people. As a whole, white people—for lots of social and historical reasons which we hope previous chapters have shown—hold greater power in British society and British churches compared to minority-ethnic people.

As the dominant group, white people have greater power to make decisions, allocate resources, shape culture and implement change. Because we have more power, we also bear greater responsibility for addressing the barriers to racial unity and justice. That said, while some of the suggestions in this chapter are things that any person can do, others require action from people in positions of greater authority within churches. This is because we need change on both the individual and institutional levels.

WHAT INDIVIDUALS CAN DO

So what can we do to advance God's vision for racial unity and justice?

Pray

It is not a cliché to say that the first thing to do is pray. Prayer is not the only thing we should do, but it is the thing we should do first and continue to do.

What should we pray?

First, praise God. Praise God for his creativity and for the richness and beauty of his creation. Praise him for the incredible diversity within the human race—of gifts, personalities, physical beauty, ingenuity, cultural expression, and insights into Scripture. Ask God to help you to appreciate this dimension of his character and his people more fully. It might also be helpful to call to mind particular people or groups that you might be tempted to undervalue, and praise God specifically for their gifts and culture. For example, you might thank God for the generous hospitality you have received from a British Indian family in your church, and how that helps you to better appreciate God's lavish hospitality. Or you might thank God for the perseverance in prayer that you see in the local Ghanaian congregation, which points you to the reality of God's power and his responsiveness to prayer.

Second, examine your heart. David's prayer in Psalm 139 is very helpful for this: "Search me, God, and know my heart; test me and know my anxious thoughts. See if there is any offensive way in me, and lead me in the way everlasting" (v 23-24). We would all like to believe that we don't harbour any prejudice against people of different skin colours or backgrounds. Some of us might react negatively when we hear the phrase "unconscious bias", because we want to believe that we are in full control of our beliefs and attitudes. However, the reality of our sinful nature, combined with the images and messages we have absorbed from our cultural contexts, means that all of us have ideas or attitudes or behaviours that can be disrespectful or harmful to other people. In addition, as we mentioned in chapter 5, Scripture is clear that sin is not always active or intentional. In Leviticus 4, we see that the sacrificial system included provision for unintentional sins, committed by individuals (v 2) and by whole communities (v 13).

So, in our individual prayers, let's ask the Holy Spirit to give us insight into our own hearts, to bring to light any attitudes or ways of thinking or patterns of behaviour that dishonour people of different ethnicities. Ask God to help you see specific things, as repentance should be specific rather than general, like "God, please forgive me if I did anything racist".

Maybe you were in a Bible study with a Black colleague, and you assumed that because of your ethnicity you had more correct theology than him or her. Repent of this assumption of superiority (Romans 12:3, Philippians 2:3-4). Maybe you have never prayed in your small group or church for equal treatment of people in the criminal justice system, despite knowing that several people in your congregation have been mistreated by police officers. Repent of this failure to bear one another's burdens (Galatians 6:2). Maybe you have only ever read and recommended Christian books by white authors. Repent of this failure to recognise the gifts and contributions of minority-ethnic people (1 Corinthians 12).

Humbly repent of the specific sins the Spirit brings to your mind, and ask for his help to change.

Perhaps you are not in a church-leadership position and you do not have direct control over what is prayed about or preached about during Sunday services. As a church member, you still have a role in bringing to the attention of those in leadership things that could and should change to make your church a more inclusive place for people of all ethnicities.

Finally, ask God for humility, wisdom and courage to actively pursue racial unity and justice.

Consider setting aside time in your calendar each week to pray for racial justice, or adding a reminder in your prayer app if you use one. Take a moment to pray right now for the things we've mentioned above.

Listen

As we continue to pray, we must also commit to listen.

In the first instance, this means listening to Scripture and what it has to say about racial unity and justice. A hallmark of evangelical faith is recognising the authority of Scripture over all areas of life. So let's live that out in this important area of racial justice and unity. In earlier chapters (particularly chapter 2), we tried to provide a glimpse of the riches of Scripture on this topic. Those of us in the majority ethnic group may never have taken time to reflect on this dimension of Scripture. For us to grow as disciples and to love our neighbours well, we need to be grounded in the beautiful vision Scripture presents of a multi-ethnic people of God, and be equipped with biblical principles of justice as we work towards that vision.

Alongside listening to the Bible itself, we should listen to theologians, preachers, and teachers from minority ethnic groups who can deepen our understanding of Scripture and of the lived experience of those from such groups. As we mentioned in the previous chapter, we as white evangelicals (like all people) interpret Scripture through our own particular cultural lens. For example, our tendency may be to approach Scripture through a very individualistic lens. We focus on correct beliefs, a personal relationship with God, and salvation of souls for heaven. While this approach is not completely wrong, it is incomplete. It largely misses the biblical themes of justice and *shalom* (a state of peace and wholeness), which are holistic and relate to whole communities rather than just individuals.

Because we are so steeped in our own culture, people of different cultures and experiences can help us to see these biblical truths and expand our vision for participating in God's kingdom. In the UK context, some of the people we personally have benefited from reading and learning from are Israel Olofinjana, Joe Aldred, Ben Lindsay, Usha Reifsnider, Wien Fung, and Azariah France-Williams. White British church leaders who have been thoughtfully engaged in multi-ethnic ministry and racial justice for multiple decades, like John Root[44] and David Bronnert, also have important insights and experience that we can learn from.

And while the American context is different from ours, there is some excellent thinking and work that we can learn from there; some of the people we have personally found helpful are Esau McCaulley, Charlie Dates, Jemar Tisby, Soong-Chan Rah, Lisa Fields and contributors to the Jude 3 Project.

In addition to Scripture and theology, we do well to listen to the voices of novelists, poets, and artists whose insights and creativity enable us to appreciate and better understand the lived reality of race. You might start with the work of Zadie Smith, Malorie Blackman, and Akala, among many others. Ask people in your own context who they are reading and listening to.

As we discussed in the chapter about BLM and CRT, listening is not the same thing as totally and uncritically accepting. But listening with humility, respect, and willingness to learn is an essential means of loving our brothers and sisters and neighbours, and seeking to understand those who are different to us (Proverbs 19:20).

Cultivate friendships

As Jemar Tisby reminds us, "People need a personal motivation to disrupt the regular patterns of racism in their lives and in society ... Relationships make reconciliation real and motivate us to act."[45]

Most of us are more likely to take action regarding an issue if we know someone personally affected by it. We are motivated to run a half marathon to raise money for cancer research after our aunt is diagnosed with breast cancer, or to write to our MP about climate change after our cousin's village is damaged by extreme flooding. With the social evil of racism, we as white people are often not moved to act if we do not have relationships with anyone affected by it. Yes, racism is embedded in structures, but ultimately its impacts are felt by individual people.

That's one reason why developing authentic friendships with people of different ethnicities is so essential. Through such relationships, we grow in understanding, empathy and willingness to sacrifice our own comfort for the sake of others.

Pause to think about the relationships in your life. Who do you interact with most at work, at church, and in your free time? Our human tendency is to be friends with people who are similar to us. It takes intentionality to build relationships with people who are different to us. Who, in your church, workplace or local community, could you make an effort to get to know? Ask if they'd like to go for a coffee and start to get to know each other!

Good friendships take time—trust is built gradually. And they are two-way. In a friendship, we want our whole person to be valued—our personality, perspective, talents, experiences and preferences. We are quick to perceive when a "friend" is pursuing our friendship just to get something out of us. As white people, we must not pursue friendship with a minority-ethnic person purely for our own benefit (that is, our education about race). We also need to recognise the fact that minority-ethnic people do not always want to talk about race or their personal experiences of racism, as that can be exhausting and even re-traumatising. That said, as a relationship develops and trust is built, we don't have to be afraid to ask how being a minority-ethnic person has shaped our friend's experiences at school or work or church. Sometimes, as white people, we can be fearful about raising the subject of race, in case we cause offence. However, in the context of a genuine trusting friendship, we can be honest about this fear with the other person.

Ultimately, good friends bear each other's burdens (Galatians 6:2). We celebrate with each other, and we also weep with each other. We take concrete action to support each other. And good friends apologise and forgive (Ephesians 4:32). There will inevitably be times in a friendship when we say or do something that is hurtful. In humility, let's apologise, ask for forgiveness and grow.

WHAT CHURCHES CAN DO

What about our churches? What can we do together to advance racial unity and justice? Let's think about the different parts of our Sunday worship and our fellowship throughout the week. If you are in the role of pastor or elder, or in another leadership position, you probably have more decision-making power over these areas. If you are a church member, you can play a key role in offering suggestions to those who have decision-making responsibilities, and in providing encouragement and feedback to those involved in making changes.

Prayer

Again, we begin with prayer. No matter what kind of church we are part of, the Sunday service includes time for corporate prayer. This is an opportunity to involve people from all walks of life, to bring before God issues impacting your local community and to show solidarity with those who are suffering. Are minority-ethnic people involved in your church's prayer team? What issues are you praying for as a church? Do you pray for racial justice?

One form of prayer that white evangelicals do not often practice is lament. One reason for this is that we are future-orientated and activist in nature. We want our congregations to jump into action, to be high-energy and to be optimistic about growth. Often we are too impatient to pause and reflect.

But the Bible is full of laments—both individual and corporate. To lament is to bring before God our community's sorrows, wounds, confusions and failures. In lamenting, we acknowledge our own limitations and our need for God's power, justice and mercy.

The realities of exclusion, exploitation and violence on the basis of race are things that we should lament. And our lament must also include repentance for our own part in racial injustice. This can be difficult for us, as most of us think of ourselves as generally good people who don't intentionally cause harm to racial minorities.

However, as we've seen, Scripture calls us to repent for unintentional as well as intentional sin (Leviticus 4). It also reminds us that sins have collective and multi-generational consequences:

> *I, the LORD your God, am a jealous God, punishing the children for the sin of the parents to the third and fourth generation of those who hate me, but showing love to a thousand generations of those who love me and keep my commandments. (Deuteronomy 5:9b-10)*

If we want our churches to contribute to racial unity and justice, we must be willing to lament the historic and ongoing harm experienced by minority ethnic groups, and repent of our church's participation in that harm.

A few years ago, Jason's church introduced a Sunday dedicated to racial justice in which the sermon, prayers and liturgy were focused on this issue. This annual event has proved to be a moving time when people of various backgrounds are invited to pray in lament and hope. You might also consider integrating into your corporate worship music that helps to express lament and a heart for justice. A starting point could be The Porter's Gate: *Lament Songs* and *Justice Songs*.

Preaching

There are several practical things that those who preach can do to advance racial unity and justice. One thing is to preach explicitly about what the Bible has to say about ethnicity. Exhort the congregation to celebrate ethnic diversity as part of God's good plan for humanity, to lament division and injustice, and to work towards the "Revelation 7:9" vision of people from every nation gathered around God's throne, praising God and the Lamb. Although this might sometimes be the main focus of a sermon, these themes are actually littered throughout Scripture. This means that there are probably natural opportunities to say something about these issues more often than we think.

A second practical step is for preachers to reflect on the authors they cite and the illustrations they use in weekly sermons (no matter what the topic is). Rather than only citing white Western European theologians, honour the insights from our brothers and sisters around the globe. In preparing sermons, you might also stretch yourself to read perspectives beyond the evangelical tradition. As evangelicals, we place a lot of emphasis on "correct" doctrine. While sound teaching is of course essential, this emphasis can sometimes lead us to dismiss perspectives that could helpfully challenge us or lend new insights.[f]

If you are preaching and you do cite a white Western theologian, be careful of valorising those who advocated racist views. For example, it may be very helpful in your sermon to include a quotation from Jonathan Edwards, but it would be wrong to introduce him as a model of piety in every area of his life because he owned slaves. It might also be worth asking if, in your context, you risk losing some people's attention by quoting him and, if so, whether a quote from a different person could work just as well.

When it comes to illustrations, pay attention to which ethnic and cultural groups you are speaking to through them. If your stories and visuals only reference musicians, authors, sports and leisure activities popular primarily

---

f For example, you might critically explore the work of liberation theologians such as Robert Beckford or Anthony Reddie, who place themselves in the Black liberation tradition in Britain. You are likely to have disagreements with elements of their theological method. But push yourself to try to understand where they are coming from, what their critiques of reformed evangelical theology are, and whether they might offer any helpful challenges or correctives to the way you have read or applied Scripture. For example, Beckford helpfully points out that white Western theology often divorces the mind from body and heart. He also calls our attention to the ways that white Western theology has often ignored social concerns that disproportionately impact Black people. These critiques should motivate us to reflect on our interpretation of Scripture and to recognise where we might need to develop a more holistic application of the gospel. See Robert Beckford's *Jesus is Dread: Black Theology and Black Culture in Britain* or Anthony Reddie's *Black Theology in Transatlantic Dialogue*.

among white middle-class people, you are probably excluding people in your pews who may not see themselves in your illustrations.

Third, churches can share their pulpits with leaders of different ethnicities and cultures. Because evangelicals value preaching so highly, we tend to be very protective of our pulpits. An unintended result might be that, if we do invite a guest preacher, it is almost always someone very like us—in social class, educational background, ethnicity and culture. If we truly want to deepen our understanding of God and his word, build relationships across divides, and encourage our congregations to pursue racial unity and justice, then we should be willing to share the pulpit.

Who could your church invite to preach, either from within or outside your congregation? Don't just ask them to preach about race and ethnicity but invite them to expound God's word more broadly.

Liturgies

All of our churches have liturgies, whether we call them that or not. Our services have particular elements and patterns that are followed each week (for example, a call to worship, confession, prayers, Lord's Supper, Bible reading, sermon, singing, notices, fellowship time). Each of these elements is an opportunity for us to orient our minds, bodies and hearts towards God; and to affirm our collective identity as the body of Christ.

It's easy for our churches to get stuck doing things a certain way because that's how we've always done them, or because a small group of people make all the decisions. Imagine how vibrant our churches could be if our liturgies drew more upon the cultures and gifts within our congregation and local community. Are there languages spoken in your church that could be integrated into the Sunday service in some way? Who is involved in making decisions about and leading the music, and how well does that reflect the different cultures in your congregation and local community? What kind of food do you serve before or after the service? Does this take into account different cultural preferences and gifts? See John Root's *Worship in a Multi-Ethnic Society* for further insights into what you might change in your church.

Small groups

We've already mentioned the importance of small groups. Refer back to chapter 5 for suggestions about how these might be used to work towards greater racial unity and justice, both in how they are formed and in what they do together.

Staffing and leadership

Research has shown that it is almost impossible to cultivate meaningful ethnic diversity and inclusion in a congregation without ethnic diversity in leadership.[46] So, if our churches are serious about reflecting the biblical vision of a multi-ethnic worshipping community, we need to prioritise building a diverse leadership team.

This will, of course, look different depending on the size and location of your church. As a general principle, it makes sense to aim for a leadership team that reflects the diversity of your local area.

Diversity in leadership is not merely about featuring different skin tones on stage but about sharing power and changing culture. Some church leaders have encouraged use of the word "intercultural" rather than "multicultural" to help us move towards congregational life characterised by active learning and appreciation of and exchange between cultural groups.[47] Churches that have been homogenous for a long time often struggle to take this step. This isn't necessarily because they are opposed to increasing diversity on their leadership team but because the networks through which they recruit leaders tend to be very homogenous. In the case of recruiting staff, it may be necessary to intentionally build relationships with schools, Christian camps and festivals, theological-training institutions and charities that are outside our existing networks. This can be a slow process, requiring humility, perseverance and a genuine desire to partner with people, rather than simply inviting them to implement our own vision. Where possible, actively seeking mentorship from a person of a different ethnic background can be extremely valuable.

Building a more diverse team might not require external recruitment. It is likely that there are people within your existing congregation who have gifts and the potential to lead but perhaps have not been recognised, encouraged or trained. Are there volunteers who could take on greater responsibility? Are there young people in your congregation, particularly young minority-ethnic people, who could be mentored and given opportunities to serve the church with their gifts?

What not to do!

Here it's also worth mentioning a couple of things to avoid. We need to be careful to avoid virtue signalling. One example of this would be putting out a statement about our commitment to racial justice on our church Facebook page during a week when racial injustice is in the headlines. While it is not wrong to do this, it lacks integrity if it is not accompanied by a plan for further action. Virtue signalling might make us feel that we've done something and therefore that we can feel good about ourselves. However, it does nothing to actually change the situation. It will also lead to frustration and disappointment among minority-ethnic members of our congregations if they perceive that our commitment to racial justice is superficial and self-centred. Another thing to avoid is commissioning a committee to write a report about racial inclusion, only for it to end up on a shelf. Sadly, the commissioning of reports can be a way of delaying or obscuring the need to take concrete action over how things are done in our small groups, sermons, budget meetings and hiring processes. While fact-finding can certainly be valuable, we should not think our job is done when the report has been written; the work continues.

CHURCH INVESTMENT IN OUR COMMUNITIES

If we are committed to working towards racial unity and justice, this should be reflected not only in how we treat fellow church members but also in our churches' engagement with our wider community.

Stewarding our financial resources

One way that we demonstrate love for God and for our neighbours is through our finances. Every church has a budget. Some have big budgets and some are operating on a shoestring. But no matter how much or little we have, we are called to steward it with wisdom and generosity.

If your church has a missions budget, think about how you might ensure that that money is promoting racial unity and justice. Take a look at the people and organisations you currently support. Where is your money going? Could you support an evangelical ministry that is tackling racial injustice? Could you partner with a church led by minority-ethnic people? Could you allocate part of your budget towards ministry-training bursaries for minority-ethnic students? Involve people from different cultures in this decision-making. It is important to do all that you can to avoid reinforcing the idea that majority cultures know best. But with care, small steps can be taken.

We can also think about our church's operations budget. Where do we buy our coffee from? Who do we hire to cater for events? Who do we employ as tradesmen or for special projects? Are there opportunities to support minority-owned businesses in our local communities? These might seem like small decisions, but God calls us to faithfulness in the big and small decisions. How we approach our budgets and our suppliers matters to God and is another opportunity to love our neighbours.

If your church has its own building, think about how you could share that space during the week to build relationships and support people of different backgrounds in your community. Could you offer space for free or at a reduced rent in your building to a start-up company? Could you co-host a community fair promoting local businesses? Could you launch a mentoring programme for young people in your community?

Supporting local schools and institutions

In Jeremiah 29, God commanded his people, who were in exile, to seek the peace and prosperity of the city in which they found themselves (Jeremiah 29:7; see also Galatians 6:10). One way our churches can do this is by investing in various ways in the institutions in our local area. Particularly if you live in an area where people experience the negative effects of racism and other social ills, think about how your church could be a blessing. Is there a primary or secondary school near you? If so, approach the leadership of the school to ask how your church might support their work. There may be opportunities to provide mentoring or tutoring, run holiday clubs or after-school activities, offer work placements and do assemblies or other things that the school proposes. Your church might also be near a community centre or library or small business that you could participate in or support in some way. Celebrating and investing in your local community can be a powerful way to build relationships with people across ethnic divides, learn what matters to people, demonstrate God's love, and work towards a more just and welcoming community.

Getting informed about local and national issues

Finally, our churches can make an effort to educate ourselves about local and national issues that disproportionately impact minority ethnic groups. In our church sermons or seminars or retreats, at some point we are likely to hear teaching and prayer related to abortion, transgender issues, and religious freedom. However, those of us in white-majority churches are probably less likely to hear any teaching or prayer about the mistreatment of racial minorities in the criminal justice system, immigration policy, or the need to address educational inequalities. These are issues that matter for people's lives—particularly the lives of our non-white brothers and sisters in our local and national contexts. Is there scope for us to read about them, teach about them, and pray about them in our churches?

TAKE THE FIRST STEP

We've covered a lot of ground in this chapter. Some of these suggestions are straightforward and can be put into practice straight away. Others require significant time, energy and commitment.

None of us can do everything described in this chapter, but each of us can, and must, do something. Exactly what that looks like will depend on our context, but we mustn't use the complexity of these issues as an excuse for not doing anything about them. Sticking to the status quo will always be our default if we aren't intentional about change. Yet we worship a Saviour who laid aside his privileges and used his power to serve the weak, and who calls his followers to do the same (Philippians 2:5-8).

Will you prayerfully and humbly consider what it would look like for you to advance the biblical vision for racial justice and unity? What steps will you take?

QUESTIONS

- Do you have any close friends of an ethnicity different to yours? How could you begin or strengthen relationships with people different to yourself?

- Think about the books you have read over the last few months or year. How many of these books were written by minority-ethnic authors? What two books could you read next to broaden the voices you are listening to?

- What is one part of your Sunday services that could change to better reflect God's heart for racial unity and justice?

- What is one way your church could invest some of its resources in racial justice?

- Are you willing to sacrifice some of your own comfort in church for the sake of racial justice?

7. WHAT CHANGE LOOKS LIKE FOR MINORITY-ETHNIC PEOPLE (JASON)

A friend of mine often says, "There is something incredibly perverse about those who face racism being expected to be the architects of their own emancipation". It's a little bit like women being asked to end sexual discrimination.

All of us have agency. All of us are called to use our agency to advance the flourishing of our brothers and sisters. But within our particular contexts, certain people have more cultural and institutional power than others. I am writing as a member of the Church of England. In my denomination, white British people have historically held much greater influence and decision-making power than minority-ethnic people. In my view, this means that white British people bear significant responsibility for taking actions that work towards racial justice in the church. I recognise that other denominations, particularly some Black-majority churches, have different histories and different approaches to racial justice. For those of us who find ourselves within a minoritised group[g] in our church, the pursuit of racial justice and unity can feel like an uphill battle. It can be exhausting and discouraging to be asked repeatedly for our opinions, without having the authority to turn them into action.

If you are from a minoritised ethnic group and in a position of major decision-making in your church, then rejoice! You are in a privileged position and are called to steward that position wisely. You may wish to also consider some of the suggestions outlined in chapter 6.

This chapter is about the choices and actions that all people from minority ethnic groups, regardless of our position in a church, can make. What does it look like to pursue and participate in change when we are in the minority?

LAMENT

I make no apology for addressing again an issue that came up in chapter 6. For those who have experienced hurt, frustration, denial and more, lament can be a lifeline. In his kindness, the Lord has provided language to use to lift our thoughts to him in our grief, pain and struggle. When we can't find the words, we can reach for the ones that he has given us. Psalm 94 is one of many that captures the emotions that I have needed to express when racism has come up close and personal:

---

g "Minoritised" refers to the idea that while being the global majority, in certain contexts such as the UK, the societal structures cause minority ethnic groups to face prejudice and disadvantage.

Who will rise up for me against the wicked?
  Who will take a stand for me against evildoers?
Unless the LORD had given me help,
  I would soon have dwelt in the silence of death.
When I said, "My foot is slipping,"
  your unfailing love, LORD, supported me.
When anxiety was great within me,
  your consolation brought me joy. (Psalm 94:16-19)

Lament also helps us to vocalise our pain in community with others. For example, on our Racial Justice Sunday, which we launched recently at church, we asked people who had personally experienced racism to pray. They poured out their hearts using the language of lament and gave us the opportunity as a congregation to "mourn with those who mourn" (Romans 12:15). We didn't simply brush over their pain and pretend that being a Christian made everything ok. Instead, we cried out for justice, we sought God for survival and we begged for deliverance. We slowed down and remembered together that before the day of triumph, we struggle in the days of trial.

Whether it is in a conversation, a Bible study or some other setting where you find yourself talking about issues of racism, a lament is a way of letting others into your pain with words that God has given us. Why not suggest that people pray or sing these words with you? One useful resource on this topic is a book called *Prophetic Lament* by Soong-Chan Rah.

PRAISE

As we unpacked in chapter 2, our ethnic diversity is a divinely intended reality. All of us have to suppress our own cultural preferences at times in order to love those we are relating to. But when we are feeling the exhaustion of having to do that in a more profound and persistent way as part of everyday life, we can praise God that he is the author of our difference. His design was for ethnic diversity to be celebrated, even if that is not always acknowledged by those around us.

Our family loves the song "God made me and you," by Christian hip-hop artist Shai Linne. It is such a joyful children's song that gives us a chance to celebrate our differences in a fun way that we can all engage with. This is just one example of the kinds of precious resources that are, wonderfully, becoming more and more common.

At the time of writing, I have just been teaching Ephesians 2 to some young Black men who live on our estate. It describes those who have put their trust in Jesus as God's masterpieces (Ephesians 2:10, NLT). These guys were blown away as we meditated on this! Despite often being told day to day that they were worthless, these men heard that God's verdict on them in Christ was completely different. We were able to praise God together for his countercultural verdict on us when so often we feel undervalued and overlooked.

REPENT

We, too, need to examine our hearts, for areas where

we may need to repent. Prejudice against those who are different from us is not a one-way (e.g. only white on Black) thing.

Racism towards other ethnic groups

For example, in my own church context I realised recently that sometimes those with South-East Asian heritage were being ridiculed by others in racially offensive ways. Because the instigators were mainly occasional attendees who were not professing faith, people from the congregation—myself included—had been reluctant to call out their behaviour. The reality was that I had colluded with this racism by letting it continue. I was grateful for the opportunity at one of our Racial Justice Sundays to publicly repent of allowing this behaviour to continue and to be reconciled to my brothers and sisters. Given that, in this case, the sin was observed publicly by many, it seemed fitting that my apology was observed publicly as well.

Racism within our own ethnic group

We can also be prejudiced against others in our own group. Racism tends to be experienced more acutely the darker someone's skin is.[48] A female friend of mine with dark brown skin experiences a level of prejudice and overt racism far beyond what I have—even from others with brown skin. This is known as colourism. We can buy into a kind of hierarchy of skin tone which means that the closer you are to white, the more acceptable you are. This is a sad legacy of racism that means that even Black X-Factor winners can be told to bleach their skin to get ahead in the music industry, and lighter-skinned minority-ethnic people can be suspicious of those with darker complexions.[49]

Another issue can be how class intersects with race. I have been aware of situations in which my accent and clothing has caused me to be snubbed by other Black and brown people who think that I have somehow sold out. I have been considered by white and Black colleagues alike as "not black enough", by which they mean that I am not what they stereotypically think a Black person should look, speak and act like. The same thing can happen the other way round, with those from a certain ethnic group wanting to distance themselves from those they consider to be of a lower social status than themselves.

We must repent of all such attitudes, resolving to move towards and stand alongside those with darker or lighter skin, or who are from a different social class, rather than distancing ourselves and making distinctions.

Silence instead of speech

Finally, a friend of mine has talked about her collusion with a "conspiracy of silence" on issues of race. What she meant was that in the past she had remained silent when issues of racial injustice were going on around her. I can relate.

When we are aware that we have not spoken up when we could have—by, for example, pointing out an offense that left people feeling bruised—there is an opportunity to say sorry to God and to resolve to act differently in the future.

SPEAK UP

If those in the majority group tend to bear the weight of responsibility for listening and acting, those in the minoritised group often tend to bear the weight of responsibility for speaking the truth in love about racism. This is particularly the case when many in the majority culture are simply oblivious to it.

When to speak

The book of James was written to a church that was struggling to remain unified. There seems to have been a tendency among these Christians to allow external differences to influence how they behaved towards each other.

James does not hesitate to speak up, not only about the evil of individual partiality (James 2:1-11) but also the reality of systemic oppression caused by power imbalances (5:1-6). He publicly denounces the behaviour of those who have abused their status in order to oppress those who are more vulnerable. "Look!" he says: "The wages you failed to pay the workers who mowed your fields are crying out against you. The cries of the harvesters have reached the ears of the Lord Almighty" (5:4). This is aimed at those outside the church but clearly indicts those within it who practise the same things.

James' example shows us that it is right to name injustice. We will need to consider the context and our own emotional capacity to do this at any point, but it is right to speak out.

When to be silent

To be clear, racism is not the only injustice Christians should talk about and not every instance of prejudice needs to be called out. The writer of the book of Proverbs counsels us:

Fools show their annoyance at once, but the prudent overlook an insult. (Proverbs 12:16)

It is so sad when I hear of white people who are terrified of speaking out about issues of race, or even of simply speaking to friends and colleagues of a different heritage, for fear of saying the wrong thing and being pounced on for making a mistake. We must continue to cultivate an atmosphere of love and forgiveness in our conversations that takes away that kind of fear.

Speaking and sanctification

Nevertheless, it is hard for any of us to grow in holiness if others do not from time to time point out our sin. This should be a normal part of Christian culture. We all sin in many ways (James 3:2) and yet...

Better is open rebuke than hidden love. Wounds from a friend can be trusted, but an enemy multiplies kisses.
(Proverbs 27:5-6)

Whoever turns a sinner from the error of their way will save them from death and cover over a multitude of sins.
(James 5:20)

I am grateful for those who have taken the time to lovingly and gently point out my sin. I have been greatly helped by those who have attended seminars I've given on ethnicity and have graciously raised points of disagreement or clarification. At the same time, when pastors in the networks I've been part of have asked me about my personal experiences of racism and my experience of the culture of their churches, I've sought to honestly and lovingly point out where their blind spots might be.

Speaking as service

However, there are other times when I haven't spoken up and now I wish that I had, and have therefore missed opportunities to serve others.

When the royal couple Meghan and Harry had their first son, a Christian friend of mine breathed a sigh of relief when they saw the first photos of the baby. When I asked them why, they said that they had been anxious that the baby would have dark skin. It seemed that, for them, to be royal was to be white. From the straightforward manner in which they said this to me, there was clearly no awareness on their part that this might have been problematic!

At the time, I let it go. The cost of engaging on the issue and creating discomfort in our relationship felt unnecessarily high. Sometimes that may well be the case. However, looking back, I think on balance that this was an incident where I should have asked them what they meant. Having examined myself and taken the plank out of my own eye (Matthew 7:3-5), I wish I had tried to gently point out how the comment could have been quite upsetting to some people. Instead of serving my

desire for ease, I could have served not only my friend—
by pointing out their sin—but also other brothers and
sisters, by helping to protect them from hearing that
same sort of comment on another occasion.

Speaking on behalf of others

When speaking out, we do need to acknowledge that we
can't be expected to represent all minorities—or even
all those with the same ethnic background as us. As we
discussed in chapter 3, our ethnicity intersects with our
gender, age, education, skin tone and a whole host of
other things. There is a very real sense in which my view
is simply that—one view among a variety of minoritised
voices.

However, in another sense, there are some common ways
in which minority groups in majority white culture tend
to experience reality. Let's just be transparent about what
we know for certain is experienced by many in our context
and what is merely our own opinion.

That said, there is real benefit in minority-ethnic people
advocating for brothers and sisters from different
minority backgrounds.

I chatted through this chapter with a colleague of mine,
Wien Fung, a specialist in cross-cultural mission from
a South-East Asian background. He said that East and
South-East Asians, especially migrants in the UK, tend to
be silent and conflict avoidant on issues like social justice,
advocacy and racism. He said that the impact of shame,

the instinct for survival and the discomfort with difficult conversations that might impact our collective harmony can be obstacles to addressing racial justice issues. His solution was fascinating. He wondered if those who have walked further and for longer, for example Black churches, could empower, become allies with and raise their voices with their Asian brothers and sisters. In other words, could speaking up be seen as something we do *together as a group* rather than just something we do ourselves, especially for those for whom communal values are the lens through which they see things.

GET EMOTIONAL SUPPORT

I have mentioned the need to be very aware of our own emotional capacity to speak up and to persevere. I know some friends who have effectively run out of emotional capacity, having regularly experienced prejudicial treatment, and who have pointed things out, only to find that the issues kept resurfacing and were not addressed.

It is worth thinking through what we can put in place to help provide the support network that we need. I am grateful for friends who are happy to pick up the phone and chat. I am grateful for those who have convened forums where minority-ethnic people can share feelings without fear of misunderstanding or recrimination. I am grateful for thoughtful people from the majority culture who prepared safe spaces during question times, which meant that aggressive and destructive comments (particularly during online meetings) could be filtered out, protecting us from unnecessary pain. This will look different for different people, but having a support network in place is crucial.

PRACTISE SABBATH

Another helpful way of maintaining our emotional capacity for speaking about race is by practising Sabbath. In the Old Testament, the Sabbath was a day of complete rest from secular work, following six days of labour (Exodus 20:8-11). Scholars disagree as to exactly how this continues into the New Testament, but the principle of taking one day a week to gather for worship and to rest from our labours is still a wise and healthy pattern of life.

Working for change in these areas of injustice can feel relentless and tiring. Sabbath is not simply about relaxation. It's a way of regaining perspective on our identity and role in God's world. We step back from our saviour complex, and we are forced to rely on him afresh. Practising Sabbath might look like setting aside the work for justice and refusing to send the emails about issues concerning race on a Sunday. Instead, we take time to remember who God is as we gather with our church and rest with Christian friends and family.

As my colleague Wien Fung reflected on what I had written in this chapter, he offered some wisdom that I found deeply profound: "The practice of Sabbath might just be one of the most distinctive dimensions of our work for justice that sets Christians apart from others. In practising Sabbath, we learn to know that we have done enough, we have enough and we are enough." While non-Christian society says, "Fight for your rights," Sabbath reminds us that God has bestowed on us a royal status that we do not have to prove or earn, and that means we can rest.

DEAL WITH ANGER

There is a tension that I feel I have to constantly navigate. If I speak out about race, I am an angry Black man who conforms to the racial stereotype of being aggressive, uncultured and intimidating. If I don't, I feel guilty for not saying what needs to be said if attitudes are ever going to change. This is an ongoing struggle and one which requires each of us to discern wisely what seems best.

However, there are times when anger can become an issue. As I have talked more openly about racism, I have had to relive traumatic events. I've become more aware of the difficulties that many minority-ethnic people face that others are often oblivious to. It can be frustrating when people around me seem to dismiss or even deny that this is a widespread reality. When you add in an acute awareness of the many racist acts that have happened in history, we can end up feeling overwhelmed and bitter. How should we deal with that kind of anger?

A right response

It is worth saying that sometimes anger is the right response. In fact, a lack of anger is not necessarily a sign of godliness. It can be a sign of the opposite. Jesus was angry at the Pharisees' stubborn accusations (Mark 3:1-6). He was indignant at his disciples for turning children away (10:13-14). He was so enraged at what was going on in the temple that he "began driving out those who were buying and selling there" (11:15). He didn't simply keep the peace when the God-like response in the presence of evil was wrath and anger (Psalm 69:24, Revelation 19:15). In fact, it is because God's anger is so real that his mercy is so precious.

A wrong response

The danger with our anger is that these emotions can master us in a way that they never did Christ. I have sometimes found myself facing questions at the end of a seminar and have struggled to keep my cool.

In the extreme, there are times when *being heard by others* can translate into thinking that *others should not be heard*. I'm thinking here of what is sometimes called "cancel culture"—in other words, seeking to silence (and often humiliate) the voices of those whom we disagree with. James gives us wise advice when he says:

> Everyone should be quick to listen, slow to speak and slow to become angry. (James 1:19)

In practical terms this might look like asking three questions:

1. Is this conversation about race a dialogue or monologue?

Being "quick to listen" might look like asking, "Am I genuinely willing to listen and learn and, if necessary, be corrected?" Essentially, this is about humility. There may well be lots that we can and should bring to discussions on race. But none of us have the whole picture. We need each other. In my denomination, minority-ethnic people have often been disregarded and disrespected. In the past, church doors were literally shut in their faces. More recently, I have heard many stories of people being told that they cannot preach because of their accent or that there are only certain places in the country where they can work as a vicar and be accepted. But none of this means that all of my white colleagues should be silenced, disrespected or disregarded. As brothers and sisters in Christ, we should strive to be quick to repent and quick to forgive (Ephesians 4:32).

2. How can I plan and pray about the best way of saying things?

Being "slow to speak" recognises that we can speak in ways that don't build up others. I've been grateful for times when I've delayed replying to emails containing questions about race to allow some time for reflection. The result has been much more productive conversations!

3. How can I avoid responding aggressively?

Being "slow to become angry" includes thinking about the tone we use to express even righteous anger. Harsh words tend to make it harder to be heard. To be clear, it is not that we need to avoid saying hard things—but we should be cautious about saying them in a harsh way.

Recently, it became clear that certain Black boys from our youth group were being stopped and searched weekly by the police on their way home. Youth workers had witnessed this and made formal complaints. It was easy to feel deeply frustrated and to want to blurt out that anger unhelpfully towards the authorities. What the police had done, as far as we could discern from the facts, was wrong. And yet our good and righteous anger could easily have become aggressive and unhelpful.

I was grateful that we took time to reflect, to pray with the young people and to bring the situation to our church prayer meeting so that everyone could share our distress and search for the wise way to move forward. We opened our youth provision later into the evening when the searches were happening, we walked people home, and we taught them about how God cares deeply about justice.

Despite all this, it was difficult for us to see how this situation would be resolved in a way that brought justice, with regards to the police, for these young men. In the end, like Jesus, we had to entrust ourselves to the God who judges justly (1 Peter 2:23).

SANCTIFY YOUR CULTURE

Vince Bantu, an assistant professor of church history at Fuller Seminary in America, helpfully describes how the gospel both embraces our culture and transforms it.[50]

On the one hand, as people become Christians, the truths of the gospel become absorbed into and expressed within their own cultural ways of doing things. On the other hand, as citizens of heaven we find ourselves having to step out of our culture when it conflicts with Jesus. Not everything in every culture is good, and Bantu helpfully asks us to consider Jesus' Great Commission, to "make disciples of all nations", as including both *groups of people* and *the value systems of those groups*. He calls this "cultural sanctification"—shaping our cultural expressions so that they come under the lordship of Christ.

All cultures see the truths of the gospel from a limited perspective, like watching a football match from a certain point in the stands with a restricted view. At half time we can move around and can see what the view is like from another person's seat. We can't fully experience it the way they do, but we see more clearly the limitations of our seat and the benefits of the other. In the same way, part of growing as a Christian is to see the blind spots in our own cultural perspectives and the benefits of other's. We are not expected to sit in a different seat, but we will, perhaps, become less convinced that we have the best seat in the house.

As I spend time with believers from different cultures, I see how, for example, my Korean friends take prayer a lot more seriously than I do. I see how my Ugandan friends seem to cling to joy in suffering in ways that I am slower to do. I see how my own upbringing and culture can sometimes prize information but lack joy. In other words, I am seeking to be open to how God has blessed other cultures with different insights and clearer perceptions of the gospel than I have. I am trying to see the weaknesses in my own cultural conditioning.

As a Bible teacher, I've started routinely consulting commentaries that bring a more global perspective—to open my eyes to perspectives that I would miss from my limited viewpoint.

This is also why being part of a church of many cultures can be so spiritually helpful. In a white-majority church, for example, the cultural idols of privacy and independence around money are likely to be unchallenged, because giving is rarely preached about or done with a physical basket. In an South-Asian-majority church, the cultural idol of marriage and children is less likely to be challenged. When people from different cultures are part of the same church, these kinds of differences are noticed and have to be wrestled with.

BE PATIENT

It is striking in James 5 that, immediately after calling out oppression in verses 1-6, James calls the church on the receiving end of that injustice to be patient, stand firm in faith and avoid grumbling:

> Be patient, then, brothers and sisters, until the Lord's coming. See how the farmer waits for the land to yield its valuable crop, patiently waiting for the autumn and spring rains. You too, be patient and stand firm, because the Lord's coming is near. Don't grumble against one another, brothers and sisters, or you will be judged. The Judge is standing at the door! (James 5:7-9)

The church James was writing to faced deep-seated

problems that would not be resolved overnight, so a huge degree of patience was needed. The same is true today.

I confess to finding this hard to hear. It feels as if this point could let majority cultures off the hook. It feels particularly hard because in my experience, issues around racial justice are always *theoretically* very important but *functionally* of little importance. When it comes to choosing how to spend our money or our time, or deciding what to do with our church programmes, issues of race are often not quite important enough to make the cut. If they do make the cut, they get a very carefully controlled segment which is quickly forgotten.

As we have said before, a celebration of ethnicity and stamping out of racism are not the only issues that we must wrestle with in our Christian communities. It would be wrong to think that a church should expend all of its energy addressing this one area of discipleship and injustice. Nevertheless, these issues hit me hard because I cannot escape them. I cannot forget about them once the seminar is over, or the Bible study finishes, or the guest preacher leaves.

Because of this, I am grateful for James' reminder to remember how our story ends. Christ will bring justice when he returns:

> *Brothers and sisters, as an example of patience in the face*
> *of suffering, take the prophets who spoke in the name of*
> *the Lord. As you know, we count as blessed those who have*

persevered. You have heard of Job's perseverance and have seen what the Lord finally brought about. The Lord is full of compassion and mercy. (James 5:10-11)

Christ is coming to bring the abundance, satisfaction and wholeness that we all long for. Before then, like farmers, we must wait (v 7-9). The picture of a farmer waiting for the seasonal rains is powerful because it often feels to me as if there are times when the world becomes intensely interested in and sensitive to the area of racism; but those times are quickly followed by long periods where very little seems to be happening as a result. I'm sure that that is how farmers felt between the rainy seasons—abundance was followed by drought. They had to trust that, in the end, the harvest would come.

The promise for us is that, whether or not we see progress now, Christ will bring peace in the new creation. Part of his bringing peace will involve passing judgment—so I don't need to take out my anger on others. Christ is a far more perfect judge than me. And because he sees all our hearts perfectly, only those in Christ will stand. None of us can naturally stand in his holy presence.

Finally, James reminds us that all those who suffer stand in the company of great heroes who have persevered through trials to see "what the Lord finally brought about" (v 11). So hang on to this reality. Change may be painfully slow in us and in our communities. We may be misunderstood and may misunderstand others many times. We may need to keep forgiving and asking for forgiveness.

Yet we hold on to the promise that "people will come from east and west and north and south, and will take their places at the feast in the kingdom of God" (Luke 13:29); that people "from every nation, tribe, people and language [will be] standing before the throne and before the Lamb," in a forever celebration (Revelation 7:9).

And that our great slain Shepherd will lead us to everlasting springs of water as he wipes away every tear from our eyes.

QUESTIONS

- How have you processed your emotions around racism in the past? Could using biblical laments help?

- What are the challenges you have faced as a minority-ethnic person when it comes to speaking up about racism? How has this chapter affected your thinking?

- Have you observed healthy ways of dealing with anger caused by racism? What was it about them that stood out?

- In what ways do you think that your culture might need to be "sanctified"?

APPENDIX:
TWO PERSPECTIVES ON RACISM

There are two common ways of framing the problem of racism, both inside and outside of the church. In chapter 5 we call them the "structural perspective" and the "individual perspective". Given the impact that failing to see the validity of the other point of view can have on everyday relationships, we've taken some time to describe those two views in a little more detail here. As we will see, both perspectives have merit and some biblical support. The issue is that many of us, influenced by sin, tend to view the problem so exclusively through one frame that we struggle to see other ways in which specific racial problems need to be addressed. If one perspective tends to dominate in a particular church, any challenge to this can feel (and be received as) strange and untrue.

THE STRUCTURAL PERSPECTIVE
This approach sees racism as primarily a structural problem. In other words, it is social institutions and processes

that perpetuate the problem of racism. Because these institutions and processes are embedded in our everyday lives, the problem of racism is large and often unseen.

It is not that there are a few bad apples who simply need a bit of education in order for the problem to go away. It is a pervasive problem that requires wholesale structural change. Since the processes in place tend to favour the status quo, there is little incentive for major change. Therefore, the key means of addressing the problem is a redistribution of power.

Structuralists will also tend to frame things in terms of oppressors and oppressed groups. Caring about oppression is entirely biblical. After all, the Lord told Moses he would redeem his people because he saw "the way the Egyptians are oppressing them" (Exodus 3:9). He is "a refuge for the oppressed" (Psalm 9:9). He counts oppression of the marginalised as akin to sorcery and adultery (Malachi 3:5; see also Ezekiel 22:29). But the paradigm of oppressors and oppression may not capture all the complexities of dealing with racial prejudice, as chapters 3 and 4 have tried to unpack.

The structuralist approach tends to be preferred by the minority culture, who are always much more aware of everyday racism and the ways in which racism is pervasive and often unconscious.

As we have seen in chapter 3, there is precedent for this kind of approach in Acts 6. In that situation, a church mercy ministry seemed to be biased against a certain ethnic group. Structural change in the leadership was needed to address the problem.

One of the important things that this passage highlights is that knowing and hearing the gospel isn't always enough on its own to solve the problem of racism. These were spirit-filled believers who had seen first-hand at Pentecost that the gospel message was for all people. And yet, in their church practice, they either deliberately or inadvertently allowed a process to emerge that neglected a certain ethnic group. The key, though, is that, once identified, this discriminatory practice was addressed through structural change.

However, more negatively, the structural approach tends to downplay individual agency or responsibility. There is often little sense that an individual might bear some responsibility for their circumstances or actions. As a result, people from the minority culture holding this view can adopt a victim mentality that discourages them from seeking to take steps to change their circumstances. Likewise, those from the majority culture holding this view may assume that their commitment to structural change means that they do not need to also examine their own hearts and personal behaviour.

THE INDIVIDUAL PERSPECTIVE

This approach sees racism as primarily a problem of individuals. It is the result of the poor behaviour of a few. The general progress that we have made in society in living well with one another means that a few bad apples are the exception to the rule. The problem of racism is largely solved, as evidenced by our legislation on racial equality and the success of individual minority-ethnic individuals (for example, Priti Patel as Home Secretary, Rishi Sunak as Chancellor of the Exchequer and Lewis Hamilton as one of the most successful Formula One drivers of all time). People who are racist behave in obvious and often extreme ways that are easily observed and obviously wrong—for example, the offensive insult or the racialised attack.

"Individualists" will tend to see the solution to racism as a combination of education and legislation. Those who behave badly simply need to be educated as to the wrongness of their behaviour. The progress that we have already made in equality legislation needs to be reinforced. Because most of this is already in place, there is no significant problem to be dealt with—or at least, not one that requires drastic action. This means that the real issue at hand is to silence the conspiracy theorists who insist that racism is a bigger problem than it actually is.

This approach will tend to be favoured by the majority culture, who are less aware of the racist attitudes and actions that many minority-ethnic people have to deal with every day. The individualistic nature of Western Christianity, with its emphasis on personal conversion and personal ethics, may also lean in this direction too.[51]

There is biblical precedent for the individualist perspective as well. As we have discussed in the introduction, James 2 points out the sin of partiality. This is the attitude of treating some people prejudicially, purely on the basis of their external appearance. Like the community in Acts 6, James doesn't assume that this issue will automatically be dealt with by the preaching that Jesus Christ is Lord. It needs to be called out and dealt with as a specific sin within church life, in the same way that he addresses anger and greed.

One of the weaknesses of an over-reliance on this perspective, however, is that it will minimise the long-term, cumulative effect that sin can have on institutions,processes, attitudes, and outcomes. While the slave trade was abolished in Britain in the 19th century—not least due to the work of Christian campaigners—the belief that Black people are of a lower status can still linger in society. For instance, the last re-run of *The Black and White Minstrel Show* on the BBC—a show that by definition asserted that it is better for a white person to portray a Black person than for a Black person to portray themselves—was aired in 1978.[52] The touring version toured continuously until 1987—in other words, still well within living memory.[53]

The individualist perspective also tends to ignore the fact that sin is not always deliberate or active. In the Bible, unintentional sins still need to be dealt with and confessed (Numbers 15:22-31; Psalm 19:12). That is why each week in the confession we use our churches, we confess that we have sinned against God and one another, "in thought and word and deed, in the evil we have done, and in the good we have not done, *through ignorance*, through weakness, through our own deliberate fault" [emphasis added].[54]

You can read more about the implications of where people lean in regard to these two perspectives in chapter 5. Ultimately, though, we can eradicate sin neither by educating the individual nor by changing who is in power—if we could, God wouldn't have needed to send his Son to die for us. So, we must continue to proclaim the truth and grace of the gospel, even as we take practical steps against injustice.

GLOSSARY OF KEY TERMS

These terms are marked in **grey** the first time they appear in the book.

Anti-racism: actively fighting against racism rather than passively claiming to be "not racist".

Black Lives Matter (BLM): a global organisation and also a diffuse social movement, both focused on campaigning for racial justice.

Critical Race Theory (CRT): an academic framework within legal studies that focuses on the ways in which racial discrimination is embedded in laws, systems and institutions.

Culture: a set of beliefs, values, practices, styles and narratives that provide people with a sense of meaning and belonging.

Ethnic group: people who share a sense of common heritage, culture, or language.

Institutional racism: ideas, attitudes and actions that become embedded in our institutions so as to systematically disadvantage some racial groups while giving an advantage to other racial groups.

Justice: treating people with dignity and respect, protecting the rights of the vulnerable, and holding to account those who cause harm.

Minority-ethnic individual: in the UK context, a person who does not identify as white British.

Race: a socially constructed way of categorising and ranking people based on visible physical characteristics.

Racism: ideas, attitudes and actions that perpetuate the beliefs that racial categories are real, that some races are superior to others, and that individuals can be reduced to racial categories.

White privilege: in this context, a collection of unearned advantages that is passed on from one generation to the next.

Woke: actively alert to and informed about injustice.

FURTHER READING

Global commentaries

ESV Global Study Bible

Africa Bible Commentary by Tokunboh Adeyemo

Understanding honour and shame cultures

3D Gospel by Jason Georges

Misreading Scripture with Western Eyes by Brandon J. O'Brien and E. Randolph Richards

Theology of race

From Every People and Nation: A Biblical Theology Of Race (New Studies in Biblical Theology) by Daniel Hays

The Christian Imagination: Theology and the Origins of Race by Willie Jennings

African Voices: Towards African British Theologies edited by Israel Olofinjana

Reading While Black by Esau McCaulley

Exclusion and Embrace: A Theological Exploration of Identity, Otherness and Reconciliation by Miroslav Volf

Dynamic Diversity: Bridging Class, Age, Race and Gender in the Church by Bruce Milne

Multicultural church

Mission-shaped Church in a Multicultural World by Harvey Kwiyani

Leading a Multicultural Church by Malcolm Patten

Pursuing racial justice in the church

We Need to Talk about Race by Ben Lindsay

How to Fight Racism by Jemar Tisby

Social and historical analysis

Black and British by David Olusoga

Natives: Race and Class in the Ruins of Empire by Akala

Divided by Faith: Evangelical Religion and the Problem of Race in America by Michael Emerson and Christian Smith

Fiction

(These are a selection of books that we have enjoyed that, to different extents, touch on issues of race.)

Noughts and Crosses by Malorie Blackman

White Teeth by Zadie Smith

Americanah by Chimamanda Ngozi Adichie

Resources for children on identity and ethnicity

God Made Me and You: Celebrating God's Design for Ethnic Diversity by Shai Linne

Creative God, Colorful Us by Trillia Newbell

Black and British: A Short, Essential History by David Olusoga

The Color of Friendship—A Disney film based on a true story of a friendship that forms between two teenage girls (one Black from America and one white from South Africa during Apartheid).

Online Resources

Black and British: A Forgotten History—David Olusoga (BBC iPlayer)

Noughts and Crosses—based on Malorie Blackman's novels (BBC iPlayer)

Jude 3 Project (https://jude3project.org/)

Out of Many, One People—John Root's blog (https://johnroot.substack.com/)

Tim Keller's 4-part blog on racial justice (https://quarterly.gospelinlife.com/)

ACKNOWLEDGEMENTS

"And let us consider how we may spur one another on toward love and good deeds."
Hebrews 10:24

Writing a book often begins with feeling like a pleasant stroll through a beautiful new park and ends feeling more like the final stages of a marathon in a desert! One of the things that keeps you going in a marathon (so we're told) is the encouragement from the crowds.

In the process of writing this book, there have been many individuals who have been the "voices in the crowd" for us, spurring us on to complete the good work that we pray that this book will be for the people of God. It is a joy to honour them here.

I, Jason, would first like to thank my wife, Rachel. She often sees more clearly in the early exciting stages what the decision to write will look like later on. Yet she has been a long-suffering sounding board and support, while bringing much wisdom of her own into the conversation. Without her generosity of spirit in the midst of our busy family and ministry life, this book would not have been written.

I am grateful too for the insights of my daughter Evie, who conveyed her own reflections and the insights of her peers with clarity, patience and thoughtfulness.

It was a phone call, out of the blue from Glynn Harrison, who had been a conversation partner as I worked on a previous book, who spurred me on my journey of thinking, researching and speaking on this subject. I'm thankful for his encouragement.

Particular thanks go to Dr Matthew Mason at London Seminary, who was a regular conversation partner as I mulled over some of the ideas in the early stages. He pushed me towards greater clarity and theological depth in encounters filled with love and laughter.

I am indebted also to colleagues at London City Mission, particularly Felix Aremo and Wien Fung, who both read and fed back helpful insights on various parts of the book later on.

Finally, I praise God for partnership in this project with Jessamin and her husband, Jonno. Jessamin's sociological expertise, intellectual curiosity, incisive mind and penchant for nuance expanded my point of view and softened my sharp edges. But most of all, our collaboration has embodied the very thing that we were seeking to model: listening, dialogue, deepening inter-ethnic friendship and a passion for justice.

I, Jessamin, want to begin by thanking my parents, Doug and Jeanine. Through their friendships and the way they give and receive hospitality, they have showed me the richness of cross-cultural fellowship. Through their work with Asian Access and the Lausanne movement, they have modelled to me faithful, humble, collaborative participation in the global body of Christ.

As a student, my thinking and experience of multi-ethnic Christian community were shaped by friends and staff within Harvard's InterVarsity Fellowship. Particular thanks to Tina Teng-Henson, who mentored me and challenged me.

For my sociological training, I am indebted to Bob Wuthnow, whose consistent guidance and thoughtful feedback have been invaluable.

In the process of writing this book, I have been so grateful for Jason's theological insight, practical wisdom, encouragement and sense of humour. It has been a pleasure and a privilege to work together on this project and learn from each other's experience and perspective.

Finally, I want to thank my husband, Jonno. He has patiently and generously served as a sounding board, editor and cheerleader. The countless cups of coffee he made for me have directly fuelled this project.

We thank Rachel Jones at the Good Book Company for her tireless efficiency and attention to detail. For both of us, God has been the rock we have needed to rest on. Through the challenges of COVID, the ups and downs of personal circumstances and the impact that racism has had on our worlds in various ways, the name of the Lord has been our strong tower. In our weakness we have known his strength. When we have felt surrounded by troubles, we have known him surrounding us. And so to him goes all the glory.

REV. DR JASON ROACH AND DR JESSAMIN BIRDSALL

ENDNOTES

1 https://www.genome.gov/genetics-glossary/Race (accessed on 17 Feb. 2022).

2 For an example of how racial categories vary between nations, see Anthony Marx, *Making Race and Nation: A Comparison of South Africa, the United States, and Brazil* (Cambridge University Press, 1997); Aimable Twagilimana, *The Debris of Ham: Ethnicity, Regionalism, and the 1994 Rwandan Genocide* (University Press of America, 2003); or Neil MacMaster, *Racism in Europe 1870–2000* (Red Globe Press, 2001).

3 Sir William Macpherson of Cluny, *The Stephen Lawrence Inquiry: Report of an Inquiry*.

4 Wendy Williams, *Windrush Lessons Learned Review* (Crown Copyright, 2020).

5 Klas Rönnbäck, "On the economic importance of the slave plantation complex to the British economy during the eighteenth century: a value-added approach," *Journal of Global History*, 2018.

6 Willie Jennings, *The Christian Imagination: Theology and the Origins of Race* (Yale University Press, 2011).

7 Smedley and Smedley, *Race in North America: Origin and Evolution of a Worldview* (Routledge, 2018).

8 Sally Tomlinson, *Education and Race from Empire to Brexit* (Policy Press, 2019).

9 Race Disparity Audit (Crown Copyright, 2017), p 23.

10 Race Disparity Audit (Crown Copyright, 2017), p 37.

11 Office for National Statistics, *Household wealth by ethnicity, Great Britain: April 2016 to March 2018* (2020), p 6.

12 Joe Aldred, *Respect: Understanding Caribbean British Christianity* (Epworth Press, 2005); Anthony Reddie, *Black Theology, Slavery and Contemporary Christianity* (Ashgate, 2010).

13 John Stott, *Issues Facing Christians Today, 4th Ed*, (Zondervan, 2006), p 287.

14 https://www.linnean.org/learning/who-was-linnaeus/linnaeus-and-race (accessed on 17 Feb. 2022).

15 "A Biblical Theology of Kingdom Diversity", https://www.youtube.com/watch?v=c-FxL0rX1RY (accessed on 31 August 2021).

16 John Stott, *The Message of Ephesians*, The Bible Speaks Today series (IVP, 1979) p 153.

17 https://ctbi.org.uk/call-to-address-racial-injustice-by-cte-presidents/ (accessed on 17 Feb. 2022).

18 Jessica Nicholas, *God Loves Justice: A User-Friendly Guide to Biblical Justice and Righteousness* (S&E Educational Press, 2017, Kindle Edition), p 4.

19 Timothy Keller, *Generous Justice: How God's Grace Makes Us Just* (Hodder & Stoughton, 2012).

20 Jessica Nicholas, *God Loves Justice*, p 15.

21 "Demands", Black Lives Matter UK, 2021, https://ukblm.org/demands/ (accessed on 30 Jun. 2021).

22 "Black History Month", UK Parliament Hansard, 20th October 2020, https://hansard.parliament.uk/commons/2020-10-20/debates/5B0E393E-8778-4973-B318-C17797DFBB22/BlackHistoryMonth (accessed on 30 Jun. 2021).

23 Kimberlé Crenshaw et al, *Critical Race Theory: The key writings that formed the movement* (The New Press, 1995), p xiii.

24 "We recognise that these issues are part of a political and economic system which is reliant on the exploitation and control of Black and other oppressed people. We understand that these systems of power are global, and exist due to centuries of colonialism. We are part of a flourishing anti-racist movement which is fighting back against white supremacy and all forms of oppression." "About", Black Lives Matter UK, 2021, https://ukblm.org/about/ (accessed on 30 Jun. 2021).

25 John Calvin, *Institutes of the Christian Religion, Vol 1* ed. John T McNeill, trans. Ford Lewis Battles (Westminster John Knox Press, 1960, Kindle Edition), 2.2.16, p 523.

26 E.g. (1) "Black Lives Matter UK is a national, member led, anti-racist organisation fighting to end structural racism", https://ukblm.org/; (2) "We believe we can create a world without systemic violence and exploitation, where all can live full and free lives", "About", Black Lives Matter UK, 2021, https://ukblm.org/about/ (accessed on 30 Jun. 2021).

27 David Shepherd, "Is there 'systemic racism' in Britain? Two views (ii)", Psephizo, 27th June 2020, https://www.psephizo.com/life-ministry/is-there-systemic-racism-in-britain-two-views-ii/ (accessed on 1 Jul. 2021).

28 Crenshawe et al, *Critical Race Theory*, p 23.

29 "About", Black Lives Matter UK, 2021, https://ukblm.org/about/ (accessed on 30 Jun. 2021).

30 https://ukblm.org/ (accessed on Sep. 2021).

31 This framework is adapted from an article by William Murrell: "Critical Theory as Method, Metanarrative, and Mood," Mere Orthodoxy, 3 May 2021, https://mereorthodoxy.com/critical-theory-mood/ (accessed 30 Jun. 2021).

32 Richard Delgado and Jean Stefancic, *Critical Race Theory: An Introduction* (Third Edition) (NYU Press, 2017, Kindle Edition), p 3.

33 Delgado and Stefancic, *Critical Race Theory*, p 8.

34 Delgado and Stefancic, *Critical Race Theory*, p 10.

35 Delgado and Stefancic, *Critical Race Theory*, p 10.

36 Crenshaw, *Critical Race Theory*, p xiii.

37 Andy Crouch, *Culture Making: Rediscovering Our Creative Calling* (IVP, 2013), p 26.

38 O. Khan F. Shaheen, *Minority Report: Race and Class in Post Brexit Britain* (Runnymede Trust, 2017) p 25.

39 https://www.premierchristianradio.com/Topics2/Life/Lifestyle/The-great-divide-Can-we-reunite-a-segregated-Church (accessed on 3 Oct. 2021).

40 https://www.theguardian.com/world/2016/dec/02/middle-class-church-of-england-failing-listen-poor-bishop-burnley (accessed on 3 Oct. 2021).

41 David W. Bebbington, *Evangelicalism in Modern Britain: A History from the 1730s to the 1980s* (Unwin Hyman, 1989), p 2-17.

42 Harvey C. Kwiyani, *Mission Shaped Church in a Multicultural World* (Grove Books, 2017), p 16.

43 Herman Bavinck, *Our Reasonable Faith*, translated by Henry Zylstra (Baker Book House, 1956), p 240.

44 *Building Multi-Racial Churches* (The Latimer Trust, 2020), or his blog, Out of Many, One People

45 Jemar Tisby, *How to Fight Racism: Courageous Christianity and the Journey Towards Racial Justice* (Zondervan, 2021), p 88.

46 Michael O. Emerson, *People of the Dream: Multiracial Congregations in the United States* (Princeton University Press, 2008).

47 Ben Aldous, Idina Dunmore and Mohan Seevaratnam, *Intercultural Church: Shared Learning from New Communities* (Grove Books, 2020).

48 Ellis Monk, "The Unceasing Significance of Colorism: Skin Tone Stratification in the United States", Daedalus, 2021; Ellis Monk, "The Consequences of 'Race and Color' in Brazil", *Social Problems*, 2016.

49 https://news.sky.com/story/x-factor-winner-alexandra-burke-says-she-was-told-to-bleach-her-skin-12011209 (accessed on 17 Feb. 2022).

50 V. Bantu, *A Multitude of All Peoples* (IVP Academic, 2020), p 229.

51 Michael O. Emerson and Christian Smith, *Divided by Faith: Evangelical Religion and the Problem of Race in America* (Oxford University Press, 2001), p 76.

52 https://www.bbc.com/historyofthebbc/100-voices/people-nation-empire/make-yourself-at-home/the-black-and-white-minstrel-show (accessed 26th September).

53 "Scotland's racist role: How minstrel shows spread stereotypes through country's theatres", https://www.dailyrecord.co.uk/news/scottish-news/big-read-how-minstrel-shows-11300746 (accessed on 26 Sep. 21).

54 https://www.churchofengland.org/prayer-and-worship/worship-texts-and-resources/common-worship/common-material/new-patterns-12 (accessed on 17 Feb. 2022).

thegoodbook

COMPANY

BIBLICAL | RELEVANT | ACCESSIBLE

At The Good Book Company, we are dedicated to helping Christians and local churches grow. We believe that God's growth process always starts with hearing clearly what he has said to us through his timeless word—the Bible.

Ever since we opened our doors in 1991, we have been striving to produce Bible-based resources that bring glory to God. We have grown to become an international provider of user-friendly resources to the Christian community, with believers of all backgrounds and denominations using our books, Bible studies, devotionals, evangelistic resources, and DVD-based courses.

We want to equip ordinary Christians to live for Christ day by day, and churches to grow in their knowledge of God, their love for one another, and the effectiveness of their outreach.

Call us for a discussion of your needs or visit one of our local websites for more information on the resources and services we provide.

Your friends at The Good Book Company

thegoodbook.com | thegoodbook.co.uk
thegoodbook.com.au | thegoodbook.co.nz
thegoodbook.co.in